Richard Saul Ferguson

Carlisle

Richard Saul Ferguson

Carlisle

ISBN/EAN: 9783744731836

Printed in Europe, USA, Canada, Australia, Japan

Cover: Foto ©Thomas Meinert / pixelio.de

More available books at **www.hansebooks.com**

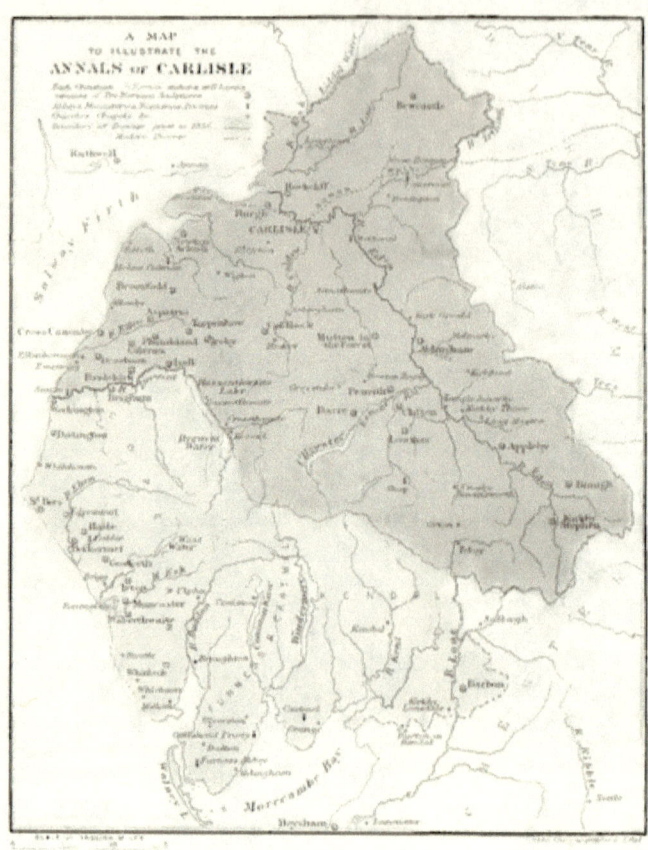

DIOCESAN HISTORIES.

CARLISLE.

BY

RICHARD S. FERGUSON, M.A., LL.M., F.S.A.,

CHANCELLOR OF CARLISLE.

WITH MAP.

PUBLISHED UNDER THE DIRECTION OF THE TRACT COMMITTEE.

LONDON:
SOCIETY FOR PROMOTING CHRISTIAN KNOWLEDGE,
NORTHUMBERLAND AVENUE, CHARING CROSS, W.C.;
43, QUEEN VICTORIA STREET, E.C.
BRIGHTON: 135, NORTH STREET.

NEW YORK: E. & J. B. YOUNG & CO.
1889.

TO THE

RIGHT REV. HARVEY GOODWIN, D.D., D.C.L.

ETC. ETC. ETC.

THE REVERED SUCCESSOR
OF THE LONG ROLL OF BISHOPS RECORDED HEREIN,

THIS

𝔥𝔦𝔰𝔱𝔬𝔯𝔶 𝔬𝔣 𝔱𝔥𝔢 𝔇𝔦𝔬𝔠𝔢𝔰𝔢 𝔬𝔣 ℭ𝔞𝔯𝔩𝔦𝔰𝔩𝔢

IS RESPECTFULLY DEDICATED

BY HIS FAITHFUL SERVANT,

RICHARD S. FERGUSON,
CHANCELLOR OF CARLISLE.

PREFACE.

So many chartularies and manuscripts relating to the history of the Diocese of Carlisle are still unprinted and unindexed, that the work of its historian must be largely attentative, and he must expect in course of time to be set right on many points.

I have to express my thanks to my friends, the Rev. T. Lees, F.S.A., the Rev. W. S. Calverley, F.S.A., the Rev. H. Whitehead, and the Rev. J. Wilson, for much valuable assistance. I have availed myself to the fullest of Archdeacon Prescott's valuable contributions to local history, and I wish there were more of them. I have pillaged without mercy the Transactions of the Cumberland and Westmorland Antiquarian and Archæological Society. I have borrowed much from the works of Stubbs, Freeman, Green, and Froude.

The wood-blocks are lent by the Cumberland and Westmorland Antiquarian and Archæological Society.

August, 1889.

CONTENTS.

Chapter		Page
I.	Introductory	1
II.	The Britons and the Romans	6
III.	Strathclyde	25
IV.	The Land of Carlisle	42
V.	The Norman Bishopric	59
VI.	The Scottish Wars	81
VII.	A Century and a Quarter of Bishops	100
VIII.	The Reformation	108
IX.	The Troubles, the Restoration, and the Revolution	138
X.	The Eighteenth Century	164
XI.	The Nineteenth Century	186
XII.	Miscellanea	205
XIII.	Archæological	219
	Index	236

CARLISLE.

CHAPTER I.

INTRODUCTORY.

THE present diocese of Carlisle consists (1) of the county of Cumberland, with the exception of the parish of Alston; (2) the county of Westmorland; and (3) that portion of the Hundred of Lonsdale, in the county of Lancashire, which is known as Lancashire North of the Sands, and which is separated from the main body of that county by the intervention of the county of Westmorland and the estuary of Morecambe Bay.

Prior to the year 1856, the diocese of Carlisle was the smallest in England, the whole of it being comprised in one archdeaconry, that of Carlisle. Its limits defined the land of Carlisle, which the Red King, in 1092, for the first time made part of the English kingdom, and formed into the earldom of Carlisle: it included great part of the counties of Cumberland and Westmorland, but not the whole of either county. Henry I. completed the work of the Red King by adding the land of Carlisle to the list of English episcopal sees, as the bishopric of Carlisle. The boundaries of the see so created remained unaltered until the death, in 1856, of

Dr. Percy, bishop of Carlisle. In that year, under the provisions of the 6 and 7 William IV. c. 77, and of an Order in Council made in August, 1847, the deaneries of Copeland, in Cumberland, of Furness and Cartmell, in Lancashire, and so much of the deaneries of Kendal and Kirkby Lonsdale as were in Westmorland, were severed from the diocese of Chester, and from the great and famous archdeaconry of Richmond, formed into a new archdeaconry, that of Westmorland, and added to the diocese of Carlisle, the severed portions of Kirkby Lonsdale and Kendal being united into a new deanery of Kendal. The diocese thus consisted of two archdeaconries, Carlisle and Westmorland, and the boundary line between them was an historical one, the southern boundary of the land or earldom of Carlisle.

In 1884, a third archdeaconry, that of Furness, was formed, and the alterations then effected in the boundaries of the archdeaconries deprive them of all historical interest; and they can only for the future be defined by the lists of the parishes they contain and by reference to the map given herewith. The number and boundaries of the rural deaneries have in like manner been increased and altered. The unextended diocese of Carlisle contained four, which appear in the register of Wetheral as Gillesland, Cumberland, Allerdale, and Westmorland, a very curious division, which must relate back to the period when, as we shall see hereafter, Gillesland was in the diocese of Hexham. A more convenient division was found in Carlisle, Cumberland, Allerdale, and Westmorland, names which appear in the *Taxatio* of Pope Nicholas; in the last century these names were discarded for Carlisle, Penrith, Appleby, and Wigton. The portion added to the old diocese of Carlisle in 1856 contained also four, which have been already named, viz., Copeland, Furness, Cartmell, and Kendal. There are now in the modern diocese nineteen deaneries. The unextended diocese of Carlisle contained 137 benefices; the present diocese contains 292, namely, 142 in the archdeaconry of Carlisle, 90 in the archdeaconry of Westmorland, and 60 in the archdeaconry of Furness. The patronage of fifty of these benefices is in the Bishop of Carlisle in right of his see; he has also the alternate patronage of two others; twenty-nine are in the patronage of the dean and chapter of Carlisle; and thirty-six in the patronage of the trustees of the Earl of Lonsdale, who are also alternate patrons of two others. The patronage belonging to the Lowther family was acquired at various times by purchase, in pursuance of a fixed political policy. The rectory of Great Salkeld was from very early times annexed to the archdeaconry of Carlisle, but the connexion was severed in 1855, and a stall in Carlisle Cathedral was annexed to it in lieu. The vicarage of St. George's, Barrow, is annexed to the archdeaconry of Furness.

The exclusion of the Cumberland parish of Alston from the diocese of Carlisle may at first sight seem an anomaly, but it is not so. By all the laws of geography that parish belongs to the county of Northumberland, and to the diocese of Durham, or since 1882, of Newcastle; the anomaly is that it belongs to the county of Cumberland, to which it has access only over a *col*, whose summit is 1,900 feet above the level of the sea. This arises from the fact that Alston contained *jura regalia*, silver mines, whose profits the Crown of England found it convenient to collect through the Sheriff of Cumberland, and Alston thus became fiscally severed from the district to which, ecclesiastically and geographically, it belongs.[1]

Some little dispute there once was as to whether the small parish of Over Denton was in the diocese of Carlisle or of Durham, arising partly out of a disputed county boundary line, unless, indeed, as is more probable, the ecclesiastical dispute gave birth to the civil one.[2] It has long been settled that the parish of Over Denton belongs to the see of Carlisle, but the chartulary of Lanercost clearly shows that in the twelfth century it was reckoned in the diocese of Durham, and other records show that it was so reckoned until the end of the fifteenth century.

From the preceding summary it will be seen that the history of a portion of the diocese of Carlisle is the history of part of the diocese of Chester, or rather

---

[1] See "Why Alston is in the Diocese of Durham, and in the County of Cumberland."—*Transactions Cumberland and Westmorland Antiquarian and Archæological Society*, vol. viii. p. 21.

[2] See Transactions Cumberland and Westmorland Antiquarian and Archæological Society, vol. iii. pp. 158, 159, 160; and Bishop Nicolson's "Miscellany Account of the Diocese of Carlisle in 1703," p. 40.

of the archdeaconry of Richmond. This must be sought for in the volumes for York and Chester in this series, and from it the present writer proposes, as a general rule, to abstain; but in treating of the religious and social aspects of the old diocese of Carlisle it will be impossible to avoid occasionally overstepping its limits, particularly in regard to the Lake Country.

It has already been stated that the bishopric of Carlisle was founded by Henry I. Before taking up the history of the diocese from that time, it will be necessary to consider with some care the previous history and condition of the district which Henry the Scholar formed into the see of Carlisle.

CHAPTER II.

THE BRITONS AND THE ROMANS.

The Romans on their arrival in Britain found the country in possession of a Celtic race, called by Gibbon and by some other historians Gauls, as being a tribe of the Gauls, who inhabited the neighbouring continent; called by Freeman and others Welsh, being the progenitors of the present inhabitants of Wales; called by Dr. Todd and by the Dentons, in their manuscript histories of Cumberland, Irish; and by many called Britons, or British, as being found in Britain by the Romans. After the Romans left Britain this Celtic race was conquered, superseded, and thrust aside by a Teutonic race from near the mouth of the Elbe, Angles, Saxons, and Jutes, from whom we English are descended. Both the Celtic and Teutonic races are Aryan in origin, descended from that common stock, which has peopled nearly all Europe and great part of Asia. It seems certain that the Celts, or Celtic race, were preceded in Britain by a non-Aryan race, who were unacquainted with the use of metal, a knowledge which the Aryan race appears always to have possessed. History tells us nothing about these people, but the spade does, and it informs us that the people whose remains are found in conjunction with instruments of the stone age had skulls of a dolicho-cephalic or long-headed type, and disposed of their dead by inhumation: the same instrument also tells us that the people of the next age, the bronze age, were a round-headed (brachy-cephalic) people, who used both inhumation and cremation. The implements of the stone age have frequently been found in Cumberland and Westmorland, but it is to be noted that all those so found belong to the newer stone age, to the neolithic period. Of the older stone age, of the palæolithic period, of the man coeval with the cave hyena, the cave bear, with the woolly elephant and the hairy rhinoceros, no remains have yet, we believe, been found in either Cumberland or Westmorland in either caves or river drift.

Of the brachy-cephalic people of the bronze age fewer relics can be catalogued. Bronze celts, spear-heads, and palstaves have all been found in Cumberland and Westmorland, and if more are not on record it is due to the fact that thirty or forty years ago it was common for the brass-founders to buy them for twopence apiece and melt them. Barrows of this period have been opened in the two counties by the Rev. W. Greenwell, F.R.S., F.S.A. But of these people, the Celtic brachy-cephalic people of the bronze age, other traces remain to us in the names they gave to the country they dwelt in, and in their influence on the local dialect. Scholars have differed much as to the amount of this influence, and the curious must refer to "The Northmen in Cumberland and Westmorland,"[1] and to the "Dialect of

---

[1] London: Longman & Co. Carlisle: Steel, 1856.

Cumberland,"[1] both by Robert Ferguson, F.S.A., and to "Cumberland and Westmorland, Ancient and Modern," by J. Sullivan.[2]

Both the historians and the philologists agree that there were two waves of Celtic migration into Britain; to the earlier one belonged the ancestors of the people who speak Erse in Ireland, Gaelic in the Highlands of the North, and Manx in the Isle of Man, and are called by Professor Rhys Goidels; to the later one belonged the ancestors of the people who speak Welsh in Wales, and Breton in Brittany, and are called by Professor Rhys Brythons.[3] Traces of the language spoken by both these people can be found in the place-names of Cumberland and Westmorland, so that it is evident that both waves reached these counties; and thus we have, prior to the advent of the Romans, three peoples settled in the district whose ecclesiastical history we have to write, two Celtic and one pre-Celtic. Professor Rhys, however, in his map of Britain, showing the relative positions of its chief people during the Roman occupation, assigns the district wholly to the Goidels, with faint traces of the pre-Celtic race in the hill district.

Thus far all our knowledge about Britain has been merely conjectural and speculative: the time when we first really begin to know anything about the country is about fifty or sixty years before the com-

[1] London: Williams & Norgate. Carlisle: Steel, 1873.
[2] London: Whitaker & Co. Kendal: John Hudson, 1857.
[3] "Celtic Britain," by J. Rhys, M.A. London: Society for Promoting Christian Knowledge, 1882.

mencement of the Christian era, for in B.C. 55 and 54, Julius Cæsar made expeditions into the south of the island. There seems to be no doubt that, in the southern and maritime parts of the island, he found a state of civilisation much greater than is generally supposed.[1] The tribes that Cæsar came across were even then acquainted with the use of iron, and appear to have had a large mixture of Belgic immigrants from the comparatively civilised Gaul. This civilisation would not extend very far, and the tribes that inhabited the north and west (including Cumberland and Westmorland) would be much more barbarous than their southern and eastern neighbours; might still be using bronze or even stone implements, while iron was common to their neighbours, or even to their own chieftains and wealthy men. Cæsar speaks of the number of the population and the frequency of buildings, but this can only refer to the maritime provinces under Belgic influence: they were corn-growing countries. The wild tribes of the interior, and of the north and the west, did not cultivate the earth, but lived on milk and flesh, and clothed themselves in skins. They stained themselves with a blue dye, made from woad, to give themselves a more terrible appearance in battle, and wore their hair long, and shaved all but the upper lip. They wandered to and fro, driving their herds and flocks from pasture to pasture, but throwing up temporary dwelling-places for security to themselves and their cattle, living much as their kinsmen, the wild Irish, did

---

[1] *Vide* Evans' "Ancient Stone Implements," p. 10. Evans' "Coins of the Ancient Britons," pp. 42, 263, and *alibi*.

three centuries ago. Their dwelling-places were mere temporary establishments, formed in the forests by enclosing a space with felled trees, within which they made huts of reeds, and logs, and stones, and sheds for their cattle. Men such as these were the Brigantes, a tribe, or federation of tribes, which inhabited, probably sparsely, the mountainous and woody districts now known as Yorkshire, Lancashire, Westmorland, Cumberland, and Northumberland.

Another question arises: that is—What kind of country was that, which is now called Cumberland and Westmorland, when the Romans arrived? It was mainly forest, resembling the uncleared forests of Canada and America, and covered with dense scrub of oak, ash, thorn, hazel, and birch: the hill near St. Bees in Cumberland, known as Tomline, was at the beginning of this century covered with such scrub, high enough to hide a horse, while at the other end of the county, at Alston, the stools of ancient hazel and birch trees are buried beneath the peat. Other parts, particularly a great tract north of the present Carlisle, must have been impenetrable bog and morass, while the tops of the higher hills probably stood up bare and naked. Even in the time of Charles II. great part of Cumberland was forest, as we learn from Sandford, who about that time wrote a history of the county, which remains in manuscript.

Ptolemy, in his geography, allocates nine cities to the Brigantes; seven of these are situate to the eastward of the great central water-shed, but Galagum or Galacum, and Rigodunum have been allocated, one to or near Kendal, and the other to Ribchester, in Lancashire. Such cities were probably mere collections of miserable wigwams.

We have little information about the religion of the people of Britain. Professor Rhys, of whose interesting volume on Celtic Britain[1] we have already made large use, classifies the people of Britain, as regards religion, into three groups: the Brythonic Celts, who were polytheists of the Aryan type; the non-Celtic natives, under the sway of Druidism; and the Goidelic Celts, devotees of a religion which combined Aryan polytheism with Druidism. The epigraphy of the local Roman remains will presently serve to throw a little light on the polytheism of the Brythonic Celts.

It would be superfluous here to go into the details of the Roman conquest of Britain; an excellent summary of it has been written by Prebendary Scarth.[2] Prior to the year A.D. 78, the Romans had established themselves, more or less precariously, in the southern parts of the island. The real conqueror of Britain was Agricola, the third of three great generals sent over by Vespasian. The first of these, Petilius Cerealis, effected the reduction of the Brigantes in Yorkshire, in the years A.D. 69 and 70. Agricola came from Rome to take the chief command in Britain, in A.D. 78, and held it until 84, during which time he reduced all Britain, up to the friths of Forth and Clyde, to the condition of a

---

[1] "Celtic Britain," by J. Rhys, M.A. London: Society for Promoting Christian Knowledge, 1882
[2] "Roman Britain," by the Rev. H. M. Scarth, M.A. London: Society for Promoting Christian Knowledge.

Roman province. His first proceeding was to put to the sword the Ordovices or inhabitants of North Wales, who had been troublesome; he then reduced to entire submission the Isle of Mona, *i.e.*, Anglesey: this he did by fording the strait which separates the island from the mainland. The winter of 78-9 he spent in quarters among the Ordovices; in correcting many abuses connected with requisitions of corn and other supplies, which pressed hard upon the Britons, and seem to have been learned by the Roman officials in the school of Verres. Thus having pacified and secured the country in his rear, Agricola pushed his conquests northwards. When the warm weather of 79 came, he drew together his forces again, and started off from North Wales on a second campaign, and this time to the northwards. Where he went, the twentieth chapter of his Life, by Tacitus, tells, in the words "*æstuaria ac silvas ipse prætentare,*" words that can only apply to the estuaries of Lancashire and of Cumberland, of the Dee, of the Mersey, of the Ribble, to the sands of Cartmel and of Ulverstone, and of the Solway,—a district that has already been mentioned as well and thickly wooded, even so late as the time of Charles II. The use of the word *æstuaria* shows that Agricola crossed the rivers just mentioned as near the sea as possible, and we think that he proceeded north by the coast of Cumberland, and by a road and chain of forts which can still be made out. This we fancy he did that he might be supported by his fleet,[1] and might also avoid the trackless woods and wild mountains of the

[1] This is matter of controversy.

interior: indeed, the passes into Cumberland and Westmorland from the south are few and hard to force, defended, as they would be, by swarms of Britons, who would have every advantage of shelter and knowledge of the country. At the end of this year's campaign, he encircled the territory gained by a chain of forts, "*multæ civitates . . . et præsidiis castellisque circumdatæ.*" Tacitus, in his account of Agricola's third campaign, defines for us the limits of the second year's conquests: "*tertius expeditionum annus novas gentes aperuit,*" showing that in the second year Agricola did not get beyond the Brigantes, who were well known to the Romans, having been in Yorkshire defeated and subdued by Petilius Cerealis. Thus Agricola, in his second campaign, marched round the Cumberland coast, subduing the country up to the Solway and the Tyne, and establishing the chain of forts which stretched round the Cumbrian coast and from the Solway to the Tyne, and whose ruins still excite curiosity and admiration.

In his third year, Agricola marched as far as the Frith of Tay, and in his fourth year (A.D. 81) he drew a line of forts from the Frith of Forth to the Frith of Clyde, while in the following two years he made further use of his fleet, and campaigned north of his upper line of forts, north of which line, however, he never made any permanent conquests.[1] Agricola's

---

[1] See a paper entitled "An attempt at a Survey of Roman Cumberland and Westmorland, with Remarks on Agricola's line of march, &c.," by the Author.—*Transactions Cumberland and Westmorland Antiquarian and Archæological Society*, vol. iii. p. 64.

successors were unable to retain the northern part of his conquests, and when Hadrian came to Britain, in A.D. 120, he found it necessary to connect the line of Agricola's forts between the Solway and the Tyne by a continuous fortification, known to this day as "The Roman Wall." The military engineers who planned this great barrier had a twofold object in view; accordingly they planned the great barrier with an embattled stone wall as a defence to the north against the attacks of hordes of barbarians that might be called armies; with a palisaded earthen vallum to the south against the attacks of guerillas, banditti, and dacoits that infested the scrub and forest in their rear. Into this system the engineers incorporated most of Agricola's camps; they also provided smaller ones at intervals of about a mile for the shelter of the large guards that would have to mount day and night, and they provided a military road. For a more detailed description the curious must refer to Prebendary Scarth's "Roman Britain;" to Dr. Bruce's magnificent works, "The Roman Wall" and "The Lapidarium Septentrionale," while the visitor to the remains of the great barrier should not fail to carry with him the little Handbook the same learned scholar has provided; many valuable papers on the Roman Wall are also to be found in the Archæologia Æliana of the Newcastle Society of Antiquaries.

Antoninus Pius, the successor of Hadrian, united the upper line of Agricola's forts, those between Forth and Clyde, by an earthen barrier.

The Roman rule in Britain lasted for about 350 years, if we reckon from Agricola in A.D. 78 to

Honorius in A.D. 410, a period of time about three times as long as that during which we have borne empire in India. With the history and incidents of that period we are hardly concerned; but some brief inquiry into other matters during the Roman sway, so far as they concern the district with whose ecclesiastical history we are dealing, will be of interest.

We have already said somewhat of the condition of the country through which Agricola forced his way; it may be well here to give a picture of Britain as the Romans found it, from the pen of a master, and then to apply it locally:—

"It was a land of uncleared forests, with a climate as yet not mitigated by the organised labours of mankind. The province in course of time became a flourishing portion of the Empire. The court orators dilated on the wealth of Britannia Felix and the heavy corn-fleets arriving from the granaries of the North; and they wondered at the pastures almost too deep and rich for the cattle, and hills covered with innumerable flocks of sheep with udders full of milk and backs weighed down with wool. The picture was too brightly coloured, though drawn in the Golden Age. It is certain that the island, when it fell under the Roman power, was little better in most parts than a cold and watery desert. According to all the accounts of the early travellers, the sky was stormy and obscured by continual rain, the air chilly even in summer, and the sun during the finest weather had little power to disperse the steaming mists. The trees gathered and condensed the rain, the crops grew rankly but ripened slowly, and the ground and the atmosphere were alike overloaded with moisture. The fallen timber obstructed the streams, the rivers were squandered in the reedy morasses, and only the downs and hill-tops rose above the perpetual tracts of wood. . . . The work of reclaiming the wilderness began in the days of Agricola. The Romans felled the woods along the lines of their military roads; they embanked the rivers and threw causeways across the morasses; and the natives complained that their bodies and hands were worn out in draining the fens, and extending the clearings in the forests." [1]

The truth of this picture is testified by the numerous remains the Romans have left behind them in the district with which we are dealing. It is sad to note that the majority of the monumental inscriptions found in Cumberland and along the great barrier of Hadrian, record persons who died in youth or middle age. The effigies of the dead on their monuments indicate that warm clothing, probably of some woollen material, was worn.[2] Small camps in sheltered positions,—for instance, one in the park at Netherhall,— seem to have been *sanatoria* for men invalided from the more exposed ones. The colds and chills of the climate were guarded against by various contrivances, occasionally by double walls, as at the camp known as the King's stables, on the Poltross Burn; more frequently by elaborate systems of heating apparatus, known as hypocausts. A magnificent instance was uncovered at the Roman villa near Ravenglass. Its draught and consumption of wood must have been tremendous, showing that it was required to produce a large amount of heat. Other instances occur in most of the Roman camps in Cumberland and Westmorland. The Roman villa near Ravenglass

---

[1] "Origins of English History," by C. Elton. Quaritch, London, 1882, p. 222.

[2] Transactions Cumberland and Westmorland Antiquarian and Archæological Society, vol. viii. pp. 317, 320.

is an exception; no others have been found in the district now the diocese of Carlisle; the climate repelled the wealthy and luxurious; no tessellated pavements are on record as having been found here, and the only settlers so far north were the officers and officials of the Roman Empire. The villa at Ravenglass, from its position close to a great camp, was clearly the residence of a military commander, and all the Roman remains in Cumberland, Westmorland, and North Lancashire nestle up close to the camps, or great fortified barracks, with which the Roman dotted the land, and whose names still afford the epigraphist and antiquary ample opportunity for ingenious conjecture. The occupation of this district was a military one; nowhere within it do we find great villas, as in the south of England, far away from military stations, and surrounded by numerous offices that bespeak great agricultural operations. The Roman, during his stay in the north, probably did little for local agriculture; for horticulture he probably did more; salads and vegetables were a necessity to the Roman, and he is by local tradition accredited with introducing chives and potherbs. But he worked the mines in the district, or made the natives work them for him; the best authorities all consider that he worked the lead mines in Alston,[1] and ancient beds of scoriæ in High Furness, marking the sites of ancient iron bloomeries, are, on good ground, attributed to Roman times.[2] The Romans

---

[1] Transactions Cumberland and Westmorland Antiquarian and Archæological Society, vol. viii. pp. 7, 11.

[2] *Ibid.*, vol. viii. pp. 85, 89.

also established, it is believed, a trade in cattle between Ireland and the Cumberland ports in their occupation, and probably established the great local cattle fairs of Stagshawbank, in Northumberland; Brough Hill, in Westmorland; and Rosley, in Cumberland. Under these circumstances the Britons, who dwelt away from the Roman camps and roads, would not come much under the influence of Roman civilisation, and would retain, even down to the departure of the Roman, their own ways and manners. Luguballium, the modern city of Carlisle, was a station of great importance, though it is doubtful if it was walled with stone; we hereafter find the citizens showing its Roman remains as antiquarian curiosities to St. Cuthbert. Leland says of it :—

"In diggyng to make new buildyngs yn the towne, often tymes hath bene, and alate fownd diverse foundations of the old cite, as pavimentes of stretes, old arches of dores, coyne stones squared, paynted pottes, mony hid in pottes, so hold and mouldid that when yt was strongly touchid yt went almost to mowlde. . . . In the feldes about Caerluel yn plewhyng hath bene fownd diverse Cornelines and other stoneys wel entaylid for seals."

A temple to Mars was standing in the reign of William Rufus. Carlisle must thus have been the seat of a high degree of Roman civilisation. For accounts of the great camps at Birdoswald, at Old Carlisle, at Maryport, and elsewhere in the limits of the diocese of Carlisle; for their names, and for accounts of the roads which connected them one with another, and with the rest of Britain we must refer our readers to books on Roman Britain.[1] It is certain that Carlisle is the ancient *Luguballium;* Birdoswald, *Amboglanna;* Maryport, *Axelodunum;* Brough-on-Stainmoor, *Verteræ;* Brougham, *Brovonacæ;* and Old Penrith, *Voreda;* and it is certain that *Concangium* is nowhere near Kendal. One great trunk road ran from York to Carlisle by Bowes, Brough, Kirkby Thore, and Old Penrith: another ran from Chester over the Morecambe Sands round the coast of Cumberland, with a branch by Kendal to Old Carlisle near Wigton, while the Maiden Way ran through the Tebay Gorge viâ Kirkby Thore, Alston, Birdoswald, and Bewcastle, into Scotland.

The garrisons that held these camps, pursuant to the usual Roman policy, were drawn from various distant nations, so that in addition to Italians proper, there were settled in this district, Spaniards, Gauls, Germans, Thracians, Dacians, Moors, and many more—a motley crew, some of whom brought with them their own peculiar deities as will presently be shown.

Numerous inscriptions are found near the line of the Roman Wall, and in or near the Roman camps in Cumberland and Westmorland, addressed to the various deities worshipped by the legionary and auxiliary troops. These divide themselves into some four classes: first, those addressed to the gods and goddesses of the Roman mythology. Thus many

[1] See "An Attempt at a Survey of Roman Cumberland and Westmorland," by the Author.—*Transactions Cumberland and Westmorland Antiquarian and Archæological Society*, vol. iii. p. 64.

altars have been found in Cumberland dedicated to Jupiter, for instance, by the Dacians at Birdoswald, Lanercost, and Bewcastle; by the Tungrians at Castlesteads; by the Gauls at Old Carlisle; by the Spaniards at Maryport; by the *Ala Augusta* at Old Carlisle; and by other auxiliary troops elsewhere in the district, while many altars also occur dedicated to Jupiter by individuals. It has been noted that altars to Jupiter are generally larger and more ornate than those to other gods. Dedications to Mars are by no means so numerous: they occur at Birdoswald, Castlesteads, Old Penrith, Old Carlisle and Brougham, and there was a temple to Mars at Carlisle. Dedications have also occurred to Hercules, to Silvanus the god of hunting, to Victory, personified as a goddess, and to other deities worshipped by the Romans in their own Italy. The genii of the camps and the cohorts, and of the emperors, the nymphs of the fountains, all have their altars. The size and workmanship of these altars, particularly those to Jupiter, lead to the idea that they were inspired by the Roman commanders, and belong to an early period of the occupation.[1] The second class of these dedicatory inscriptions are to gods with strange uncouth names, the local gods of the Brythonic Celts. These altars are generally small and rudely carved, indicating a late period of the occupation, and that they were the work of the rank and file of the Roman legions and their auxiliaries who had intermarried or cohabited with the native women,

---

[1] "Lapidarium Septentrionale," p. xv.

and so become acquainted with their gods. Thus in Cumberland altars have been found dedicated to Belutucador, to Mogontis, to Vetiris, to Maponus, and to Setlocenia: those to Belutucador have also been found in Westmorland. Some have endeavoured to identify this god with the Phœnician Baal, in which case he would belong to the next class: both he and Cocidius appear joined in dedications with Mars, and so may be Brythonic gods of war. Maponus is conjoined once or twice with Apollo, and may be his native equivalent. These deities are frequent in, if not peculiar to, Cumberland, and must have been found there by the Romans. The third class consists of dedications to deities imported by the auxiliary troops. This class includes the *deæ matres*, whose altars and inscriptions are numerous in Belgic Gaul and in Germany, and especially along the banks of the Rhine. They belong to the Teutonic race, and are represented as three seated female figures, with baskets or bowls of fruit on their knees; instances occur, locally, of either dedications to or representations of the *deæ matres* at Brougham, Old Penrith, Stanwix, Carlisle, Netherby, &c. These are generally rude and poor in execution. The fourth class consists of slabs and sculptured figures, telling of the wave of Mithraic superstition that from the time of Hadrian swept from east to west. The great Mithraic find at Housesteads, in Northumberland, is outside of the district we are dealing with; but sculptured stones, indicative of Mithraic worship, have been found at Drawdikes and Murrill Hill, both near Carlisle, and at Maryport.

Little has, as yet, been done towards investigating and recording the folklore of this district; the results might curiously connect the present day with those that preceded the Romans. It might be possible to recognise in the wise men and wise women, the charmers away of disease, to whom the peasantry at the present day somewhat secretly and shamefacedly resort; the soothsayers, medicine men, and magicians of Goidelic Druidism; while the Beltain fires of the first of May may be relics of the worship of some fire god. So late as the year 1840, a large farmer at Brampton passed all his cattle through the Need fire, as a charm against the rinderpest; later still, in the Lake district, a calf has been buried alive for a similar reason, and even as we write a friend tells us that his herd advises him to bury a calf under the threshold of his byre, as an antidote to abortion among his cattle. The peasants, and better than the peasants, still believe that a holed stone hung up in a stable will avert nightmare from the horses. From what period of heathenism do these and similar superstitions descend?

No allusions to Christianity can be found on the lapidary remains left by the Romans in Cumberland, Westmorland, and Lancashire North of the Sands; and although there was, during at least the latter part of the Roman occupation, a Christian Church in Britain, it seems to have been mainly confined to the Roman towns and settlements further south than the wild districts we are dealing with, whose occupation by the Romans was purely military.

The conjecture that Christianity had penetrated

to this distant corner of Britain during its occupation by the Romans receives some support from what is recorded of the life and labours of St. Ninian. A Briton of noble parentage, his birth-place was somewhere on the shores of the Solway; whether on the Scottish or the Cumbrian side is uncertain, though some antiquaries hold there are reasons for inclining to the latter. Trained under a Christian father, he grew up to manhood distinguished for piety and zeal for religion, and he went to Italy with a view to obtaining instruction beyond that which his native land afforded. After dwelling at Rome for fifteen years, Pope Syricius sent him to Britain to spread Christianity among the people of his native Cumbria. His station as a chief's son, and his acquaintance with the native language, would be great helps to him in his work. On his way back to Britain he made the acquaintance of St. Martin at Tours, who had just instituted the monastic life in Western Europe. St. Martin instructed him in the ascetic discipline, and gave him workmen for the purpose of building a church in his own country. In returning he must have traversed Cumberland and Westmorland by the great Roman road from York to Carlisle; thence he proceeded to Whithern, in Wigtownshire, where he built the "Candida Casa," which then became the Mother Church of this district, and the *Cathedra* of its earliest bishop. Near to the Roman road just mentioned, at Brougham, in Westmorland, is the church of St. Ninian's, Brougham; and it is suggested that there, on his return journey, 200 years before the mission of

St. Augustine, St. Ninian for a short time preached the Gospel to the Britons in their native tongue, and that he afterwards sent a presbyter to take charge of the converts; the idea is so fascinating that one would wish it had a more solid historical basis. St. Ninian returned to Britain in 397, just 200 years before St. Augustine preached the Gospel to the Saxons in Kent. At Canterbury St. Augustine found an old British church dedicated to St. Martin; there was possibly a church at Brougham of as early, if not an earlier date.[1]

[1] "St. Ninian's Church, Brougham," by the Rev. T. Lees, F.S.A.—*Cumberland and Westmorland Antiquarian and Archæological Society's Transactions*, vol. iv. p. 420. "Church Dedications in Diocese of Carlisle," by Precentor Venables. *Ibid.*, vol. vii. pp. 118, 121. There is a St. Ninian's Well near Carlisle, and another, under his more popular name of Ringan, at Oldchurchland, Loweswater.

CHAPTER III.

STRATHCLYDE.

NATURALLY, from their proximity to a district bitterly hostile to Roman rule, the Roman garrisons on the Wall were maintained to the latest period of the Roman dominion; it is doubtful if they were then withdrawn. The legions themselves were withdrawn, but it seems likely that the auxiliary troops, long stationary in the same localities, often in the same forts, ultimately remained among a people with whom they must have to a great extent become amalgamated.

Whatever became of these troops, they were but of little effect against the invasions of the Picts and the Scots, the latter of whom harried the ex-Roman province, as well from their old seats in Ireland, as from their seats in Galloway and the west of Scotland. A still more formidable race of pirates infested the eastern and southern shores of Britain, known to the Romans as Saxons, and whose depredations had long ere now compelled the Romans to appoint a Warden (or *Comes*) of the march or shore exposed to the Saxon attack. These pirates were the English, a name which included three Teutonic tribes dwelling in what we know as Sleswick, namely, the Jutes, to the north of the present Jutland; the Angles, or English proper, just below them; and the Saxons on the Elbe,—the latter the best known to the Romans, who included all three under that name;

while the three leagued tribes bore among themselves the name of Englishmen,—a name unknown to the Romans, but destined to be as famous and as glorious as ever was the name of Roman.

These English invaders bestowed the name of Wealas or Welsh, that is, strangers, upon the people whom they found in Britain; and we shall use the names "Britons" and "Welsh" as meaning the same people.

The English conquest of Britain commenced about forty years after the departure of the Romans. The Romanised Britons, left to themselves, and unable to protect themselves against the Picts and Scots, hired a parcel of English adventurers from Jutland under Hengist and Horsa, who, in A.D. 449, established themselves in the Isle of Thanet.

Into the details of the English conquest of Southern Britain, it is foreign to our purpose to go.

Of the conquest of Mid-Britain and North Britain, very little is known. The estuary of the Humber was the chief gate by which they found admission: some turned southwards, and founded the kingdom of Mercia, becoming known as Marchmen between the English and the Britons. Those who turned north founded the kingdom of Deira, and met further to the north another English kingdom, that of Bernicia, founded by Ida, who, in 547, had planted his kingdom on the rock of Bamborough. The great forest between Tyne and Tees was the march, or debateable land, between Deira and Bernicia; but these two great kingdoms were united by Æthelfrith, and formed into the great English kingdom of Northumbria, which stretched from the Humber as far north as the Forth. The east of the present kingdom of Scotland up to the Forth was, and is, English ground, though now incorporated into Scotland. Æthelfrith was a great conqueror. In 603 he defeated the Scots at a place called Dægsastan, which some think to be Dalston, near Carlisle; others Dawston, in Liddesdale. In 607 he completed the English conquest of Britain by the capture of Chester, and by so doing, he separated the Britons, of what is now Wales, from the Britons to the north of them.

The English conquest was marked by great atrocity: the wealthier Britons fled across the seas; the poorer took refuge in the mountains and the forests, until hunger drove them out to be cut down. So far as the English conquest extended over Britain, it was a complete dispossession. The language of the Britons disappeared, as did their Christianity; the one was superseded by the English tongue, the latter by the religion of Woden and of Thor.

The English conquest covered the eastern part of Britain. In the western and more mountainous parts, the Britons held their ground. There was a British or Welsh kingdom of West Wales, which took in Cornwall, Devon, and part of Somerset up to the river Axe. All the land west of the Severn formed a second British or Welsh kingdom, that of North Wales, which included what we now call North and South Wales. To the north was a third British or Welsh kingdom, that of Strathclyde, which took in Galloway and the rest of the south-west of Scotland, with modern Cumberland and Westmorland, &c.,

down to the river Dee,—thus extending from the Clyde to the Dee, until Chester was taken by Æthelfrith in 607.

The British or Welsh kingdom of Strathclyde, which thus extended from the Clyde to the Dee, including the district now the bishopric of Carlisle, was separated from the English Northumbria, which extended from the Forth to the Humber, by the range of mountains running down the country and forming its backbone—the great Pennine range.

Nothing almost is known of what was going on in Strathclyde during the English conquest. One of our greatest living historians has said he could see nothing through the darkness that hung over Strathclyde. Probably Strathclyde was merely a collection of petty British or Welsh states, under different rulers, having a kingdom of Strathclyde proper, with its capital at Alcluid, or Dumbarton, whose ruler probably had a shadowy superiority over the others. Sir Francis Palgrave names the chief of these states as :—Reged, in the south-west of Scotland ; Strathclyde, or Clydesdale, and Cumbria, in the south. Mr. Freeman calls the whole Strathclyde, and that name for long overshadowed and absorbed the others ; but the double meaning of the term must be kept in mind, the extended and the restricted one. The people who dwelt in this great British or Welsh kingdom were called Cumbri, a designation we first meet with in the Chronicle of Ethelwerd,—at a much later date though than this. The Saxon Chronicle says that in 875 the Danes made frequent attacks on the " Peohtas " and on the " Stræcled

Wealas." Ethelwerd translates this passage into Latin as " Pihtis Cumbrisque."

The Britons of Strathclyde or Cumbria occupy a tolerably large space on the map, but a very small one in history ; their annals have entirely perished, and nothing authentic remains concerning them except a very few passages, wholly consisting of incidental notices relating to their subjection and their misfortunes.

Romance would furnish much more ; for it was in Cumbria that Rhyderic, or Roderic the Magnificent, is represented to have reigned and Merlin to have prophesied. Arthur held his court in Merry Carlisle, and Peredur, the Prince of Sunshine, whose name we find amongst the princes of Strathclyde, is one of the heroes of the Mabinogion, or tales of youth, long preserved among the Cymri. These fantastic personages, however, are of importance, in one point of view, because they show what we might otherwise ignore, that from the Ribble in Lancashire, or thereabouts, up to the Clyde, there existed a dense population, who preserved their national language and customs. Even in the eleventh century the Britons or Welsh inhabited the great part of the western half of the island, however much they had been compelled to submit to the political supremacy of the English invaders.

After the conclusion of the English conquest of Britain by the capture in 607 of Chester, by Æthelfrith, King of Northumbria, the character of the warfare between English and Briton changed ; it died down into a warfare against the separate British provinces, West Wales, North Wales, and Cumbria, which went on until the victories of that Edward I., who died on Burgh Marsh. To return to Æthelfrith. Æthelfrith, before his death in 617, reduced the petty states of Cumbria to some sort of tributary position, and in the reign of Edwine, King of Northumbria and Overlord of Britain, they were so much so as to be sometimes included in the name of Northumbria.

The district was very extensively colonised by English settlers from Northumberland; their settlements may be known by the termination "ton." They entered by the great roads the Romans had left, and settled right and left of these roads. One division came along the Roman Wall and its roads, and settled at Walton, Irthington, and Brampton, and turned southwards to Plumpton, and Hutton, and Newton, and filled the great central fertile plain of Cumberland to that extent that it acquired the name of Inglewood, the wood of the Angles, or English. Another lot streamed in by the Maiden Way; we find them at Alston, in Cumberland, and at Dufton, Marton, Bolton, Clifton, Helton, and Bampton, in Westmorland. In the west of Cumberland they got to Wigton, Aikton, and Oulton; in fact they absorbed the most fertile and most accessible part of the district,—that great plain which extends from Penrith, widening northwards as the mountains open out, and sweeping round westwards by the Solway. The mountains were left to the old inhabitants,—the Britons.

It is not, then, surprising that Ecgfrid, King of Northumbria, who reigned from 670 to 685, absorbed

Carlisle and a large district round it into Northumbria; in fact, he made *Carlisle and the district round it English ground, though not part of the kingdom of England,* and he bestowed a portion of it on St. Cuthbert,—for the English invaders had been converted from the religion of Woden and of Thor to Christianity. How that was done, how the heathenism of Northumbria was attacked, first, from the south by Paulinus, the missionary of the Roman Church; secondly, by Aidan and by Boisil, the missionaries of the Celtic Church; how Wilfrid of York and Benedict Biscop, on the one hand, and Colman on the other, struggled for the supremacy of their churches, and how the Roman Church, at the Synod of Whitby, won a victory, which enabled her to appoint Theodore of Tarsus Metropolitan of England, are matters of the deepest interest to us, but belong rather to Northumbrian than to Cumbrian history, and have been well told by the late Rev. J. L. Low, in the volume of this series devoted to Durham.

For the religious history of Cumbria during the period whose secular history we have rapidly run through, we must hark back in point of time, and glean what we can from church dedications and lapidary remains, in addition to what can be found elsewhere.

In our last chapter we mentioned the conjecture that the single dedication in the diocese to St. Ninian was connected with the personal ministrations of that bishop. But beyond the fact that through his preaching the southern Picts abandoned their idolatrous worship and received the pure faith, and that among them he ordained priests and divided the land "*per certas parochias*," we have no certain knowledge of St. Ninian's missionary labours among the Britons of Strathclyde or Cumbria.[1] It is open to conjecture that his labours were supplemented in the last half of the fifth century by those of St. Patrick himself: the church at Patterdale, near Ullswater (formerly Patrickdale) is dedicated to St. Patrick, and there is a St. Patrick's well near the church. There are three other supposed dedications to St. Patrick in the diocese, but that of Ousby, in Cumberland, is doubtful, and those of Bampton Patrick and Preston Patrick, in Westmorland, may have no better origin than some confusion between a former owner,—Patrick, son of Culwen, or Curwen, the great grandson of Gospatrick, son of Orme, son of Ketel, and the Celtic saint. But St. Patrick's fellow-worker and kinswoman, St. Bridget, is commemorated by no less than five dedications, all in Cumberland, viz., Bridekirk, St. Bridget's Beckermet, Brigham, Moresby, and Kirkbride; these lie near the coast, most readily accessible from Ireland, as does also one of the other churches dedicated to an Irish saint, St. Bees, dedicated to St. Bega, to whom also the church (formerly a chapel) at Bassenthwaite, is dedicated; Precentor Venables observes that—

"When we consider the short stretch of sea which divides Cumbria from Ireland, the Isle of Man forming a convenient

---

[1] "Church Dedications in Diocese of Carlisle," by Precentor Venables.—*Cumberland and Westmorland Antiquarian and Archæological Society's Transactions*, vol. vii. p. 122.

halting-place between the two, and the frequent intercourse of the two lands in early times, it is not a little surprising that the traces of Irish evangelisation should also be so scanty. This is all the more remarkable when we remember the abundant evidences of Irish missionary agency in Wales, and among the West Welsh of Cornwall."[1]

The conclusion the precentor draws is that the Christianity of Cumbria was far less vigorous and reproductive than among the other Celtic tribes. The precentor continues:—

"Passing onwards, the next group of dedications which arrests our attention are those to St. Kentigern, otherwise St. Mungo (a name which, we are told by his biographer, Joscelin of Furness, signifies *Karrissimus amicus*), the great agent in the revolution which again Christianised Cumbria, whose vast diocese,—restoring St. Ninian's decayed, but not extinct, church,—extended from the Clyde to the Mersey, and from the Irish Sea to the eastern watershed."

There are eight churches in the diocese, dedicated to St. Kentigern or St. Mungo: viz. (i.) Irthington; (ii.) Grinsdale; (iii.) Caldbeck; (iv.) Castle-Sowerby; (v.) Mungrisdale (Mungo-grisdale); (vi.) Crosthwaite; (vii.) Bromfield; (viii.) Aspatria. No other churches in England are known to be dedicated to this saint; and the eight churches we have mentioned are all in that part of the county of Cumberland which lies north of the river Derwent. The following sketch of St. Kentigern's career is by the Rev. T. Lees, in the Transactions of the Cumberland and Westmorland Antiquarian and Archæological Society,

---

[1] "Church Dedications in Diocese of Carlisle," by Precentor Venables.—*Cumberland and Westmorland Antiquarian and Archæological Society's Transactions*, vol. vii. p. 122.

compiled from the biography written by Joscelin, of Furness, which has been edited by Bishop Forbes in the "Historians of Scotland:"—

"Kentigern's grandfather is asserted to have been a heathen king in Cumbria or Strathclyde; his mother, Tenew, was a believer in Christianity, but not baptized. Being found with child, as it is stated, by Eugenius, or Ewen, King of Cumbria, she was, in punishment for her incontinency, according to the custom of her tribe, cast down in a chariot from the summit of a rock. Miraculously escaping, she was accused of witchcraft, and, exposed in an open boat, abandoned to the waves, in the open sea beyond the Isle of May. She drifted to Culenros, and, on the shore there, her son was born. St. Servanus, who was leading a hermit's life in that neighbourhood, warned by a vision, took charge of both mother and child, baptizing Tenew and bringing up her son. He called the boy Kyentyern (*quod interpretatur Capitalis Dominus*), *i.e.*, head or capital lord; and the boy's rapid advancement, not only in secular education, but also in holiness, endeared him so much to his protector, that he used to call him, as a term of endearment, "Munghu," *i.e.*, the dear friend. Tired out by the persecutions of his envious fellow-scholars, Kentigern quitted Culros, and, arriving at Carnock just in time to witness the death of Fergus, a holy hermit who dwelt there, attended to his burial rites. The body was placed on a wain drawn by two untamed bulls, who drew it of their own accord, and without accident, to Cathures, now Glasgow, and there Kentigern buried it in a disused cemetery, formerly consecrated by St. Ninian. Here Kentigern took up his abode, and, after some time, the king and the clergy of *regio Cambrensis*, the great British kingdom stretching from the Clyde southwards, along with the rest of the Christians, few, indeed, in number, met together and besought him to be their bishop. Overruling his scruples, and imploring the blessing of the Blessed Trinity, they enthroned him; and, having summoned a bishop from Ireland, after the manner of the Britons and Scots of that period, they compelled him to be consecrated. After his consecration, he visited his extensive diocese on foot, correcting his people,—the greater part of whom had apostatised from the Church,—reforming abuses, and enforcing ecclesiastical discipline. But heathenism was still strong in the land, and Kentigern was persecuted by King Morken. Even after Morken's death, his relations continued the persecution, not only seeking to entrap the man of God, but conspiring against his life; so, after the pattern of St. Paul, who fled from Damascus, Kentigern fled from the country, and betook himself to St. Dewi, Bishop of Menævia, in North Wales; and on this journey he visited this district, as you will presently hear, and collected therein a great harvest for the Lord. Settling on the banks of the Elwy, he founded that great monastery from which the see of St. Asaph derives its origin. Men of all ages and ranks pressed into it, to the number of 965. Here he worked in peace for some years, till at length the crowning mercy of the battle of Ardderyd[1] (A.D. 573) placed a Christian king on the throne of Strathclyde. Recalled to his bishopric by the new king, Redcrech Hael, or the Liberal, Kentigern obeyed the call; and, having appointed Asaph, his disciple, as his successor in the monastery and see, he returned to the north, accompanied by 665 monks, 300 remaining in Wales with St. Asaph. For thirty years after his return to Strathclyde, Kentigern carried on his Master's work, not only among the Britons, but also among the Picts. Before the close of his life St. Columba, the great founder of the Christian colony at Iona, visited Kentigern at Glasgow. They exchanged embraces, and filled themselves with spiritual feasts before they refreshed the body. 'How great,' adds Joscelin, 'was the sweetness of heavenly contemplation in their holy hearts is not for me to say, nor is given to me, or to those like unto me, to search out the hidden manna, as I think, entirely unknown save to those who taste it.' The two saints exchanged their pastoral staves; that which St. Columba gave to

---

[1] The site of this battle is generally identified with Arthuret, nine miles north of Carlisle, an important strategic position, commanding the fords of the Esk, and the road from Cumberland into Scotland.

St. Kentigern was long preserved in honour at Ripon, St. Wilfrid's church. St. Kentigern died A.D. 603, in extreme old age. . . . His body was buried, as was fitting, at the right side of the altar, in his cathedral, at Glasgow."[1]

This remarkable interview between the two great Celtic saints, St. Kentigern and St. Columba, took place shortly before the arrival in England of the great Roman saint, St. Augustine of Canterbury, who, in 597, was sent into England by Gregory the Great to convert that country to the Roman faith. It is too often forgotten that before St. Augustine set foot in England, a powerful Celtic church was flourishing in the North: some people have even imagined St. Augustine preached the Gospel on Crossfell in Cumberland, and founded the church of St. Augustine at Alston. It is needless to say he never was in the North at all, and that the church at Alston is, probably, dedicated to St. Augustine, bishop of Hippo.

To return to the St. Kentigern dedications in Cumberland, north of the Derwent, these are, probably, examples of what Bishop Stubbs has termed "proprietary dedications," by which is understood that a church or chapel was called by the name of the holy person who first built, or caused it to be built, and in connexion with whom it obtained local celebrity, and not from any formal dedication to him. These local dedications to St. Kentigern are explained by a passage in Joscelin's biography of the saint.

---

[1] "St. Kentigern, and his Dedications in Cumberland," by the Rev. T. Lees, F.S.A.—*Cumberland and Westmorland Antiquarian and Archæological Society's Transactions*, vol. vi. p. 328, *et seq.*

Joscelin, in describing the course of Kentigern's journey from his diocese of Glasgow to Menævia, in Wales, mentions his arrival at Karleolum (Carlisle), where,

> "having heard that many in the mountainous districts were given to idolatry, or ignorant of the Divine law, he turned aside, and, God helping him and confirming the Word by signs following, converted to the Christian religion many who were strangers to the faith, and others who held the faith in error. He remained some time in a certain thickly-planted place, to confirm and strengthen in the faith the men who dwelt there, in which he also erected a cross as the sign of their salvation, whence the place took the name, in English, Crossfield, *i.e.*, *Crucis Novale*, in which locality a basilica, erected in modern times, is dedicated in the name of the blessed Kentigern, which is illustrated with many miracles."

Looking at the Kentigern churches, as they appear on a map, it would appear as if the saint entered Cumberland by the Maiden Way, and followed it to its junction with the Roman Wall, and along the Wall to Irthington and Grinsdale, thence by Bromfield and Aspatria towards the coast, where he might intend to embark for Wales. At these places the Lake mountains would be full in view, and probably excited his curiosity about their inhabitants, and induced him to visit them in order,—Caldbeck, Castle-Sowerby, Mungrisdale, and Crossfield, which can be no other than Crosthwaite, the parish church of Keswick. Joscelin continues:—

> "Turning aside from thence, the saint directed his steps by the sea 'shore, and, through all his journey scattering the seed of the Divine Word, gathered in a plentiful and fertile harvest unto the Lord. At length, safe and sound, he reached St. Dewi."

St. Kentigern probably went south from Crosthwaite by the Roman road to Chester.

St. Kentigern included the district with whose ecclesiastical history we are dealing in the bishopric of Glasgow, which he founded, and which extended from the Clyde to, probably, the Mersey.

Two dedications in the diocese, both in Westmorland, commemorate St. Columba, a dedication which is rare in England.[1] It seems probable that dedications to Celtic saints were once more common in the district; the dedications of many churches in the diocese are unknown. A careful scrutiny in the wills in the pre-Reformation registers of the Bishop of Carlisle has failed to recover a single one of these dedications, and it appears probable that they were unknown at the date when these wills were made; these wills extend over the fourteenth century. If we omit from these churches with unknown dedications those that were mere chapelries to large parishes, we shall find that the remaining ones lie along or near the Cumberland coast, the place most accessible to Irish missionary work. Dearham is one of these churches; to its lost dedication a clue was found during the extensive repairs carried out in 1882. In pulling down the chancel arch the shaft of an early cross was discovered, which is thus described by the Rev. W. S. Calverley, F.S.A., then vicar of the parish:—

"In the upper part is a human figure on horseback, carrying or holding something in front on the horse's shoulders. The

---

[1] "Church Dedications in Diocese of Carlisle," by Precentor Venables.—*Cumberland and Westmorland Antiquarian and Archæological Society's Transactions*, vol. vii. p. 122.

whole is surrounded by spiral work and little bosses : beneath, a bird with long bill and short tail bears a baby or bundle in its big claws : in front of the bird a deformed man-figure holds forth a vessel in his right hand : above the man's head appears to gape a pair of jaws, which belong to the double-stemmed, spiral, worm-like bodies which surround the figures, and curl and twist into every unused space : beneath the bird is twice repeated the ancient symbol of endless existence,—the *svastica*. —now the cross sign, used in all ages, and passing, as it ought to do, into every faith, because the truth of which it tells is as old as Paradise ; and beneath these, again, the characteristic spirals of British or Celtic or Eastern work." [1]

These curious carvings represent the legend of St. Kenet, or Keneth (Kenedus), whose history Mr. Calverley thus gives from Capgrave :—

"Kenedus was son of the daughter of Diochus, a prince in Letaina, Lesser Britain, born a mile from King Arthur's palace. in the province of Goyer (Gower) : he was lame from birth *crus femori adherebat*. After baptism he was thrown into the river in a coracle, and by a great storm carried to an island, from which the seabirds bore him with claws and beaks, and placed him on a rock, where they covered him with many layers of feathers, driving the *serpents and worms* from the place. An angel descended, and placed a brazen bell to the mouth of the little one. Each day the bell was replenished with milk from a *deer* or forest doe. A shepherd, who had his house on the sea-shore, found the child in his nest upon the rock, and carried him away from the birds to his own home ; but the seagulls gathered in troops, and finally the boy was borne back to his rocky perch. Kynedus grew up,—deformed, it is true, but a holy hermit, who had learned that of food the bitterer and sharper and harder, the most pleasing to God, and, like St. David, able to live on roots and herbs. . . The rude and

---

[1] Cumberland and Westmorland Antiquarian and Archæological Society's Transactions, vol. vii. p. 291.

weather-beaten sculpture still shows plainly the seagull with its burden in its claws, the figure with the old-shaped papped bell in his right hand, and the worm things which the early saints, no less than the seagulls, are credited with having driven away."

It seems a reasonable conclusion that the church at Dearham was dedicated to St. Keneth; we have here a link between Wales and Strathclyde at an early date, St. Keneth being of the sixth century at the latest. It seems probable that the other churches whose dedications are lost might also indicate links between Strathclyde and Wales, or Strathclyde and Ireland. After the triumph of the Roman Church over the Celtic Church, dedications to saints not of the Roman Church would have a tendency to fall into oblivion.

We have now brought up the history of the Celtic Church to the same point as that to which we, a few pages back, brought up the history of the English conquest, the colonisation of the district by the English, the absorption of Carlisle and a district round it into Northumbria by Ecgfrid [670 to 685]. Ecgfrid granted a portion of this district to St. Cuthbert. The grant was made in 685: it included *civitatem quæ vocatur Luel* (Carlisle) *quæ habet in circuitu quindecem milliaria:* also *terram quæ vocatur Cartmel et omnes Britannos cum eo.* The expression *civitas* would seem to indicate that Carlisle had some political organisation distinct from that of the rest of Cumbria; that its circuit was fifteen miles shows that more was included than the mere inhabited town. Now the old parish of St. Cuthbert Without would, with the town, be about fifteen miles in circuit, and this was what Ecgfrid gave to St. Cuthbert. It occupies the angle between the rivers Eden and Caldew, and was probably the only land then cleared and cultivated in the vicinity of the town. The land across the Caldew, which afterwards became the parish of St. Mary's Without, and the land across the Eden, which afterwards became the parish of Stanwix, were both uncleared scrub in St. Cuthbert's days. By Ecgfrid's conquest a portion of Cumbria, so much as he made English ground, was transferred from the see of Glasgow to St. Cuthbert's see of Lindisfarne. We have thus the Roman traditions, to which the Northumbrian Church had after the Synod of Whitby in 664 adhered, introduced into Cumbria. The gift to St. Cuthbert of the city of Carlisle and land about it was by way of a pecuniary endowment, and not by way of conferring spiritual jurisdiction. Ecgfrid, probably by the advice of St. Cuthbert, founded a nunnery and schools at Carlisle. From the supposed figure of a nun in stone having been found under the foundations of the present church of St. Cuthbert's, Carlisle, when it was re-erected, in 1778, it has been conjectured that the nunnery occupied the site where the church now stands. The figure has long ago been lost; it is almost certain to have been no nun at all, but some Roman relic.

CHAPTER IV.

THE LAND OF CARLISLE.

SHORTLY after Carlisle and the district round it had become English ground, and part of the see of Lindisfarne, St. Cuthbert himself visited his new possessions. A day or two after St. Cuthbert's arrival, as some of the citizens were taking him round for the purpose of showing him the walls of the city, and a fountain or well, of marvellous workmanship, constructed by the Romans, he suddenly became disturbed in spirit, and leaning on his staff, he bent down his face sadly to the ground, and again raising himself up, he lifted his eyes to heaven, and groaning deeply, he muttered—" Perhaps at this very moment the hazard of the battle is over." When questioned by the bystanders, he would say no more than, " Do you not see how marvellously disturbed the air is? and who among mortals is sufficient to search out the judgment of God?"

Next day, a Sunday, he preached, and the burden of his discourse was, "Watch and Pray, Watch and Pray," which his hearers misapplied to the expected recurrence of a plague, which had recently ravaged the district. In a few days came a solitary fugitive, who announced that "the Picts had turned desperately to bay as the English army entered Fife, and that Ecgfrid and the flower of his nobles lay a ghastly ring of corpses on the far-off moorland of Nechtansmere."

Inquiry revealed the fact that the king fell on the very day and at the very hour at which St. Cuthbert bent over the old Roman fountain at Carlisle.

It would be most interesting were it possible to identify one or other of the ancient wells with which Carlisle is honey-combed, as that which the local antiquaries of the seventh century took St. Cuthbert to see: some have suggested one or other of the wells within the area of the castle, but a more probable suggestion is the old market well, now filled up and lost, which was in the roadway of English Street, opposite the shop of Messrs. C. Thurnam & Sons.

On the moorland of Nechtansmere there fell for ever with King Ecgfrid, in 685, the Northumbrian supremacy over England. Mercia at once struck for independence; Galloway arose, and chased the Northumbrian Bishop Trumwine,[1] out of Whithern, which stands, Bede says, "by the arm of the sea," *i.e.*, Solway; "which parts the lands of the English and Scots,"—proof that in 685, if not long before, the district around Carlisle had become English ground, though not part of the kingdom of England. It still remained subject to the fallen Northumbria, which had vitality enough to capture, in 756, Alcluid; and thus all Strathclyde, except Galloway,

---

[1] Trumwine was probably Bishop of Abercorn, and not of Whithern. See Haddon and Stubbs' "Councils and Ecclesiastical Documents," vol. ii. pt. i. p. 7 n. Green, in his History, makes him of Whithern.

became tributary to Northumbria, which was, however, too weak to retain its rule. The inhabitants of Strathclyde thus got left to themselves for a century or so, during which their country was the scene of much confused fighting, in which English, Scots, Norsemen, and Danes, all took part.

The weakness of Northumbria allowed that kingdom to fall an easy prey to a new race of invaders, —the Danes. Between 867 and 869 they conquered Northumbria, and dismembered it; Deira, now Yorkshire, they seized and occupied; Bernicia they made a tributary. Halfdene was the Danish leader, who, in 876, occupied Deira, and he extended his ravages into modern Cumberland. He laid Carlisle in ruins, so that for two hundred years it laid waste, and large oaks grew on its site. On the dismemberment of Northumbria by the Danes, Carlisle and the district round it, or Carliol, which we cannot doubt is defined by the diocese of Carlisle, as it existed prior to 1856, fell to neither English nor Danish rule. It turns up incorporated with Strathclyde proper, and with Galloway, under the name of Cumbria. One Grig, king or regent of Scotland, *i.e.*, of the Scots and the Picts, is said to have brought this about by force of arms; but marriage with a British princess, rather than conquest, or perhaps the two combined, must have been the cause of Grig's success. After Grig's death we find there was some relationship between the kings of Scotland and Cumbria.

Meanwhile the English and the Danes had been fighting with great vigour. Alfred the Great had commenced the attempt to reduce to English rule the territory known as the Danislagh, where Danish laws and customs prevailed. Edward the Elder, King of the English, continued the warfare, and, in 924, he wrested Manchester from the Danes, whereon the whole of the North laid itself at his feet, not only Northumbria, including the Lothians, but the Scots and Picts of Scotland; and the Britons of Cumbria chose him to be "FATHER AND OVER-LORD." The Britons of North Wales had done so before, and thus Edward, King of the English, became Overlord, or Emperor, of the Britons and the Scots. This transaction is the famous "*Commendation to England of Scotland and Strathclyde.*" Fierce has been the war of pens that has raged over it: Scottish historians can ill brook to own that, in 924, Scotland declared itself vassal to England, and their energies have been directed to the whittling away of its importance. But it was the foundation of all the claims made by Edward I. to Scotland. At the time it was of but little practical importance: the Overlord, Edward the Elder, died almost immediately. War at once broke out all over the North, and lasted, —spite of a peace made at Dacre, in Cumberland, where Bede tells us there was a small monastery,— until Ethelstan, King of the English, in 929, defeated Constantine, King of Scotland, and Eugenius, or Owen, King of Cumbria, at the battle of Bruanburgh. Eugenius, or Owen, whichever may be his name, fell in this battle, whose site is unknown.

In 945 Dunmail, "the last king of rocky Cumbria," fell out with his Overlord, Edmund the Magnificent,

King of the English, who at once fell upon Cumbria, laid the whole of it waste, and handed it over to Malcolm, King of Scotland, on condition that he would be his ally by land and sea. Tradition says that the decisive battle between the English and the Britons of Cumbria took place at Dunmail Raise, and that King Dunmail fell there. Other accounts say that he escaped, and died peaceably at Rome, some years later.

To briefly review these events, which are of great political importance in the general history of this country: King Dunmail was, by virtue of the Commendation of 924, vassal to King Edmund. He revolted against his Overlord, who took his kingdom from him and granted it, in 945, to Malcolm I., King of Scotland, as a feudal benefice in the strictest sense. *Cumbria thus became a fief of the Crown of England*, but *not a fief held within the kingdom of England; it was without that kingdom, and had always been so.*

Nothing is recorded of Cumbria for many years, except that in the year 1000 it was laid waste by the English. At this time it was the chief *rendezvous* of the Danes in Britain. It is doubtful whether the English attack was on the native Cumbrians or on the Danish settlers. This *rendezvous*-ing of the Danes in Cumbria would be the time when they made extensive settlements in the district now Cumberland and Westmoreland, which may yet be known by the termination "by." There are some sixty-three of these. Like the "tons," the English "tons," they occupy the best of the country, running in a circle from Appleby on the south-east, along the Cumberland plain to Allonby on the Solway, and cropping up again at Ponsonby.

In addition to this Danish colonisation, there was an extensive one from Norway, utterly unrecorded in history, but proved beyond possibility of cavil by the researches of Mr. Robert Ferguson.[1] The place names of the district prove it,—above one hundred end in the Norse termination of "*thwaite*"; nearly as many end in the Norse termination "*garth*" or "*guard*," or "*gard*." These names lie, not in the plain, but in the high ground avoided by the Danish "*bys*," and the English "*tons*." The *thwaites* occupy higher ground, as a rule, than the *guards*. Both lie thickest towards the west of the district, thus showing the Norsemen to have entered from the west. They came from their *depôt* in the Isle of Man, which they had seized.

The Danes and the Norsemen brought with them into the district a fresh wave of heathenism, the heathenism of Woden and of Thor.

Amid all these settlers and invaders,—English, Danes, and Norse,—the Britons or Welsh of Strathclyde, Reged, and Cumbria gradually melted into the surrounding population, and their language ceased to be discernible as that of a separate race. But that was a slow process. Their language is thought to

---

[1] "Northmen in Cumberland and Westmorland," by Robert Ferguson, F.S.A. London: Longman & Co., 1856. See also "Lakeland and Iceland," by Rev. T. Ellwood.—*Cumberland and Westmorland Antiquarian and Archæological Society's Transactions*, vol. ix. p. 383.

have lingered in secluded places until the Reformation, when it was possibly destroyed by the ministrations of the Protestant clergy. A few British local traditions still remain. Pendragon Castle reminds the traveller of the fabled Ather or Uther. Some of the mountains which adorn the landscape retain the appellations given to them by the original population, and Skiddaw and Helvellyn now rise as the monuments of a race which has passed away.

About the middle of the tenth century the English put an end to the kingdom of Northumbria, and entrusted its government to a series of Earls, of whom Siward is the best known. Siward was appointed by Edward the Confessor, and he defeated and slew Macbeth, King of Scotland, the murderer of Duncan, King of Scotland. Malcolm, son of the murdered monarch, was King of Cumbria. Either this Malcolm, or his son of the same name, was placed by Siward on the throne of Scotland, and as Malcolm Caenmore long retained both Cumbria and Strathclyde in his hands. During his reign, however, the *district of Carlisle*, that is all the *Cumbrian territory south of the Solway* (defined by the limits of the bishopric of Carlisle as it existed prior to 1856), was severed from the rest of Malcolm's dominions. The date of this is uncertain, but it would appear to be 1070, in which year, as we learn from Symeon of Durham, Gospatric, Earl of Northumberland, over-ran that district, in revenge for the devastation of Teesdale by the Scots. His son, Dolphin, was put in possession of the territory thus wrenched from Malcolm's dominions, from Cumbria.

The next authentic information we have from the Saxon Chronicle, under the date 1092 :—

"The king (*i.e.*, William Rufus) went northwards with a large army to Carlisle, where he repaired the city, built the castle, and drove out Dolphin, who had before governed that country; and having placed a garrison in the castle, returned south, and sent a great number of churlish folk thither, with wives and cattle, that they might settle there and till the land."

Thus the present boundaries between England and Scotland were established, and the district, presently to be made into the see of Carlisle, became for the *first time part of the English kingdom*, and England assumed its present geographical limits. Rufus, of course, found the site of Carlisle a ruin, a *waste chester*; it had been so since Halfdene the Dane. He also introduced a new ethnological element, Saxons from the south, and the ethnological strata in the district would seem to be Briton (Welsh), Angle, Pict, Dane, Northman, Saxon. These various ethnological strata indicate each a different religious wave. The heathenism of the Britons and the heathenism introduced by the Roman legions were bathed in a wave of Celtic Christianity, and Cumbria became a territorial part of the Celtic Church, owing allegiance to the bishopric of Glasgow or that of Whithern while it existed. The first English settlers brought in with them a heathen wave, the religion of Woden and of Thor. Over this swept another wave of Christianity, from Northumbria, bringing with it the Roman allegiance, and the Roman use, while the town of Carlisle with the parish of St. Cuthbert

Without (fifteen miles in circuit) and the district of Cartmell in Furness became by Ecgfrid's gift part of the endowments of the bishopric of Lindisfarne and Lindisfarne's successor, the bishopric of Durham. With the Danes and Northmen came another wave of the worship of Woden and of Thor, feebler, probably, than its English predecessor, and too shallow to swamp the Christianity it found before it. The Saxons imported by William Rufus were, of course, Christians, as were the other of his followers that settled in or round Carlisle, except a stray Jew or two whose names appear in the early Pipe Rolls.

We have already pressed into our services the dedications of the local churches for the period prior to the advent of St. Cuthbert in Carlisle; let us see if they help for the period between that date and the arrival of the Red King, some 400 years (A.D. 685 to A.D. 1092), during the latter half of which Carlisle, *i.e.*, Caer Luguvallium, lay a waste chester, or nearly so.

To the influence of the Northumbrian Church we may ascribe four dedications to St. Oswald, namely, Dean, Grasmere, Kirkoswald, and Ravenstonedale, and the dedication of Westward or Ilekirk to St. Hilda. Sixteen dedications in Cumbria commemorate St. Cuthbert: one of these is at Carlisle. We have seen that St. Cuthbert visited Carlisle; that he preached there. Bede tells us that he held an ordination there, and that in that city he had a meeting with his friend Herbert, the anchorite of Derwentwater, whose name is commemorated in St. Herbert's Isle, in that beautiful lake, where are still to be seen some fragments of the chapel that once bore his name.[1] It is probable that the church in Carlisle, dedicated to St. Cuthbert, was founded soon after his visit. One curious piece of evidence has hitherto been overlooked. Denton, in his manuscript History of Cumberland,[2] tells us :—

"The rectory of St. Cuthbert, in Carliell, was founded by the former inhabitants of Carliell, before the Danes overthrew the city, and by them dedicated to the honour of St. Cuthbert, of Duresm, who, of ancient times, was lord of the same for about 15 miles round Carlisle. At the first foundation of the church, every citizen offered a piece of money, a coin of brass then current, which they buried under the foundation of the church steeple there, as was found to be true at the late new reedifying of St. Cuthbert's steeple, An. Dom. . . . for when they took up the foundation of the old steeple, they found well near a London bushell of that money."

These coins of copper may have been Roman, but it would be curious if a bushel of Roman copper coin did not contain a large proportion of first and second brasses, which would easily have been recognised as Roman. The find must have consisted of Northumbrian stycas, which, prior to the Danish invasion, were of copper, or a mixed metal. The number of them points to their having been thrown in by a large number of persons, assembled at a great

---

[1] "St. Herbert of Derwentwater," Rev. T. Lees.—*Cumberland and Westmorland Antiquarian and Archæological Society's Transactions*, vol. vi. p. 338. "Church Dedications in Diocese of Carlisle," *Ibid.*, vol. vii. p. 122.

[2] Now published by the Cumberland and Westmorland Antiquarian and Archæological Society, Tract Series, No. II. p. 97. It was written in 1610.

function, such a crowd as could not be collected in Carlisle after its overthrow by Halfdene the Dane in 876; the church of St. Cuthbert, in Carlisle, must have been founded prior to that date. A fragment of a Saxon sepulchral cross, on which is the word SIGTTEDIS (supposed to be the name of a female), was found in 1857 in digging foundations for an extension to the house in the cathedral precincts now annexed to the third stall. The fragment is figured in the Archæological Journal, vol. xv. p. 85, and is assigned to the year 700. It would seem, therefore, that there was a church on this site as early as that date, and it is quite possible that St. Cuthbert himself was present when the stycas were showered into the foundations of the steeple.[1] The other fifteen local dedications to St. Cuthbert are of later date. They record the translation of the saint's body,

"when, two centuries later, in obedience to his dying command, Bishop Eardulf and his clergy, with romantic and touching faith, fled with their precious deposit from Halfdene and his savage Danes, and, in the course of their weary seven years' migrations, more than once crossed the hills and moorlands of Cumbria, and brought St. Cuthbert's body within the western confines of what was afterwards claimed as his diocese. There is a mediæval tradition of some value that wherever the bearers

---

[1] It may be suggested that this fragment belongs to the burial ground of St. Mary's parish, and proves the antiquity of a church on the site of the cathedral. Not so. The place of the find is nearer the St. Cuthbert's ground than the St. Mary's. Moreover, a church would not be, in a Celtic district, dedicated to St. Mary so early as the year 700.

of St. Cuthbert's coffin made a halt of any duration, there a church or chapel was erected bearing his name." [1]

Most of the churches under this dedication probably have this origin, and from them the Rev. T. Lees, F.S.A., has traced out the supposed route of the mournful cortège.[2] The party made an attempt to sail from Workington to Ireland, but a tempest turned the sea into blood, and drove them back: the tempest, no doubt, stirred up a submarine deposit of hæmatite iron, common there.

Other early dedications in the diocese are St. Wilfrid, one church; St. Andrew, eight churches; and St. Michael, twenty-seven. Dedications to St. Michael are very frequent in Celtic districts,

"while dedications to St. Andrew were first introduced in the northern parts of Britain."[3]

These thirty-eight local churches probably owe their foundations to dates between 685 and the advent of the Normans with William Rufus in 1092. The other local dedications, including twenty-nine to St. Mary the Virgin, are probably of later date. Professor Rees[4] attributes the introduction of this dedication into Wales to the Norman lords; they probably brought it into Cumbria.

[1] "Church Dedications in Diocese of Carlisle," by Precentor Venables.—*Cumberland and Westmorland Antiquarian and Archæological Society's Transactions*, vol. vii. pp. 122, 130.

[2] "The Translation of St. Cuthbert."—*Cumberland and Westmorland Antiquarian and Archæological Society's Transactions*, vol. ii. p. 14.

[3] Mr. Skene, cited by Precentor Venables *ut ante*.

[4] Cited by Precentor Venables. "Church Dedications," *ut ante*.

It has already been mentioned that Ecgfrid founded a nunnery and schools at Carlisle, probably at the instigation of St. Cuthbert, to whom some writers give the credit of being the founder of these institutions. There is good evidence for supposing a monastery also existed there in early times. Eadred, called Lulise from having been educated at the schools founded by St. Cuthbert there, was abbot of a monastery there; indeed, it is probable the schools and the monastery were one and the same : schools, monastery, and nunnery perished when the Danes destroyed Carlisle. The same fate must have overtaken the religious house, which St. Bega probably founded on the headland that bears her name; and also the monastery at Dacor or Dacre mentioned by Bede.

Many valuable and interesting sculptured monuments exist to this day in Cumbria, which throw light on the religious beliefs prevalent in that region prior to 1092. We have already mentioned the St. Keneth stone at Dearham. In the coped tombstones, commonly called Saxon hogbacks, we have the idea, common to various races in different parts of the world, expressed that the grave is the home of the dead; the Romans had this idea, and used it in this country, as their tombs in the York museum show. The Teuton had this idea. At Cross-Canonby, at Plumbland, at Aspatria, at Lowther, at Penrith, at Bongate Appleby, and elsewhere in Cumbria we find these coped tombstones; the world tree (*Yggdrasil*) of Scandinavian thought twines over them : their curved ends descend into monstrous jaws, the jaws of Hel, Loki's daughter,

Helmuth ; but the appearance of the emblem of the Holy Trinity, the *triquetra* among these carved allusions to Scandinavian and heathen mythology, shows that the Christian religion was overcoming the old heathenism, and that the dead man below was a Christian. We find this mingling of the emblems of two religions on many cross-shafts and fragments of cross-shafts found up and down the diocese ; we find in one instance the Hell-Wolf, Fenris, portrayed within the sort of mouldings we find on a Roman altar; on another we find, as on the hogbacks, the Christian symbols mixed up with carved legends of Loki and of Balder. Of the famous cross at Gosforth it has been well said that it is at once a pictorial religious book for the heathen Scandinavian and the Christian Northumbrian. Its general appearance at a little distance is that of a Thor's hammer on a large scale, the lower part of the shaft being polished. A closer inspection shows the whole to be an elaborately-carved Christian cross set in a socket of three calvary steps. The world Ash (*Yggdrasil*), the tree of the universe, of time and of life, covers the shaft, on which are sculptured episodes, which the Rev. W. S. Calverley, F.S.A., thus describes :—

"On the west face we have a *central Hemidall-Christ*, the incarnation of the deity, holding at bay the dread offspring of Satan, whilst Loki himself lies bound beneath, and Odin the father approaches the future. The *devil* overcome. On the south side we have a *central divine hart* triumphantly walking through the world unhurt by the slime and venom of the great worm of the middle earth or by the howling dog,—the Christ, the fountain of living waters, the incarnation of the deity who, below, rides armed to battle with, and to overcome, the world.

On the east we have a *central Thor, Odin or Baldr-Christ*, who fights the last great battle and overcomes the *flesh*, which is crucified and pierced with the spear; who, though the jaws of Hel gape wide and swallow him, in another personification,— Vidar the Silent, he who opened not his mouth before his foes,— rends asunder those very gates, victorious over death and the grave, and, as we see on the north side, rides on—the everlasting conqueror through His glorious resurrection."[1]

The episode of Loki bound also occurs on a pre-Norman stone at Kirkby Stephen Church, Westmorland; and also been recently identified upon one of the two pillars in Penrith Church, standing at head and foot of the well-known Giant's Grave.

Those who wish to go more fully into this most interesting subject of pre-Norman sculptured stones must consult the papers of Mr. Calverley, in the fifth and succeeding volumes of the Transactions of the Cumberland and Westmorland Antiquarian and Archæological Society. To Mr. Calverley is due the credit of having been the first to interpret these lapidary pages of local history, and he has kindly furnished the little table at the end of this chapter.

No inscriptions in the Ogham characters used by the Celts are known in the district; inscriptions in the Teutonic runes exist. There is one on a gravestone at Dearham Church, which Professor Stephens assigns to A.D. 850-950; it is covered with Christian symbolism, and the Professor reads the runes—

Adam,
May Christ his soul save.

---

[1] Transactions of the Cumberland and Westmorland Archæological Society, vol. vi. pp. 373, 400.

There is a runic inscription on a cross-shaft at Beckermet, which has been read to refer to Bishop Tuda, the successor of Colman, but this reading is doubtful, and the runes are probably of a later period. There is another on a font at Bridekirk, which has sculptured on it the baptism of our Saviour; this refers to one Richard as its maker: from the Bolden book he is known to have flourished about 1160. Then we have the famous cross at Bewcastle, bearing the figure of our Saviour, and runic inscriptions: this, Professor Stephens assigns to the seventh century, but Miss Margaret Stokes to a period between the tenth and thirteenth centuries, judging from its analogy to instances of early Christian art in Ireland.

APPENDIX.

By the Rev. W. S. CALVERLEY, F.S.A.

PRE-NORMAN SCULPTURES, DIOCESE OF CARLISLE.

List No. I. comprises sculptured stones of the period embracing the work of SS. Ninian and Patrick.

List No. II. covers the time of S. Kentigern, and thence we pass to Nos. III., IV., &c., to the Lindisfarne School and to sculptures containing various mythological subjects, according to the tone of thought of the natives and of the different settlers amongst them.

No. I.—White Sandstone: Generally having a boss in the centre of the crosshead, surrounded by a raised circle or by a circle of bosses. Ornamented with spiral work, often designed to show three curves together as a sign of the Holy Trinity. Also spiral work with interlacing bands, interspersed with bosses or pellets and the curved Triskele, the Svastika, and the S-shaped symbol, with scroll-work, the key pattern, or plait-work, on the edges. Drawn with a free hand:—Beckermet, Hale, S. Bees, Workington, Distington, Dearham, Cross-Canonby, Plumbland, Bridekirk, Aspatria, Bromfield, Brigham, Isell.

No. II.—Red Sandstone: Interlacings without interspersed pellets or symbols, save occasionally the Triquetra:—Irton, Waberthwaite, Muncaster, S. Bees, Beckermet, Hale, Workington, Distington, Dearham, Cross-Canonby, Gilcrux, Aspatria, Brigham, Aldingham, Hesket in the Forest, Bongate Appleby, Rockliff.

Sculptures, with Runes, at Beckermet, Dearham, Bridekirk, Carlisle.

No. III.—Red Sandstone, with mythological traces: Beckermet, S. Bees, Gosforth, Hale, Dearham, Plumbland, Cross-Canonby, Brigham, Penrith, Bewcastle, Dacre, Kirkby Stephen.

No. IV.—Other pre-Norman remains at Barbon, Lowther, Clifton, Ireby, Torpenhow, Newton Arlosh, Caldbeck.

CHAPTER V.

THE NORMAN BISHOPRIC.

THE land which the Red King added to the English kingdom was the land of Carleol, or Carlisle. Some doubt has recently been raised as to whether it was under the Red King or his successor that the land of Carlisle became the earldom, and Ranulph de Meschines the earl thereof:[1] but there is no doubt that Henry I. founded the Norman bishopric of Carlisle. This region, the land of Carlisle, was one over which various conflicting claims to ecclesiastical jurisdiction existed: the Bishop of Durham appears at the accession of Henry I. to have been in actual ecclesiastical possession of some part of the region. His title was founded, as to spiritual jurisdiction, on the conquest of King Ecgfrid, and as to certain endowments upon the gift by King Ecgfrid in 685 to St. Cuthbert of the city—

"*quæ vocatur Luel quæ habet in circuitu quindecim milliaria.*"

In times when kingdoms and bishoprics were co-extensive, Ecgfrid's conquests in Cumbria would naturally be taken to belong to the diocese of his bishop, St. Cuthbert, to the Anglian diocese of Lindisfarne to the exclusion of the Celtic Bishop of

[1] "Visitations in the Ancient Diocese of Carlisle," by J. E. Prescott, D.D., Archdeacon of Carlisle. Carlisle, 1888: C. Thurnam & Sons. Cambridge: Deighton, Bell & Co., p. 8.

Glasgow. It is probable that Ecgfrid's power in Cumbria included little more than what he bestowed on St. Cuthbert as an endowment, namely, the city of Carlisle and the cleared district in its vicinity, forming the old parish of St. Cuthbert-without-the-Walls, an area within which many field names, such as Cuddy's (Cuthbert's) close, Cuddy's chair, &c., record its connexion with the saint bishop. The rights thus obtained served as pegs on which to hang greater claims. In 854 we find from Symeon of Durham, that Eardulf, bishop of Lindisfarne, claimed Carlisle:—

"*Eardulphus. . . . cathedræ pontificalis* [*Lindisfarne*] *gubernacula suscepit, nec minorem quam proximis Lindis-farnensium quibusque longe positis Episcopatus sui locis pastoralis curæ sollicitudinem impendebat: quorum Luel, quod nunc Carleol appellatur, non solum proprii juris Sancti Cuthberti fuerat, sed etiam ad sui Episcopatus regimen ab Ecgfridi Regis temporibus semper adjacebat.*"[1]

From the wording of this passage it would seem that Eardulf laid claim to Carlisle for two reasons, namely,—that it [and as much of Cumbria as Ecgfrid conquered] was laid to his bishopric in the time of Ecgfrid, and belonged to his *regimen*, and that it was part of the endowment [*proprii juris*] of the see by Ecgfrid's gift; the *regimen* and the *proprii juris* being different things, one extending over a larger area than the other, the last having its boundaries fixed by Ecgfrid's gift, the first varying originally as the boundaries of the Northumbrian supremacy over

[1] *Ante, p.* 40.

Cumbria varied, but afterwards probably able to maintain a hold in places from which the Northumbrian supremacy had receded. Eardulf's successors at Chester-le-Street and Durham, after Lindisfarne ceased in 875 to be a see, continued their claims to jurisdiction and probably to emoluments in the land which Ecgfrid had made English. The well known *Veredictum Antiquorum*, in the cartulary of Lanercost, concerning the chapel of Triermaine in Gillesland, says :—

"*Gilmore filius Gilandi qui erat dominus de Treverman et de Torcrossoc fecit primum unam capellam de virgis apud Treverman et procuravit divina in ea celebrari (Dom. Edelwano Episcopo concedente). Enoc tunc persona de Walton, pro quadam parte terre que nunc vocatur Kirkland unde sacerdos et clericus suus possent sustentari, ad ministrandum et serviendum in predicta capella. Et Gillemor, dominus de Treverman admisit ad illam capellam serviendum Gillemor, capellanum consanguineum suum, qui primum hospitabatur in terra predicta et ipsum herbergare fecit multo tempore ante adventum Huberti de Vallibus in Cumberland.*"

Edelwan, or Edelwyn, was bishop of Durham, 1056 to 1071, and we here have him exercising jurisdiction in the land of Carlisle before the advent of the Red King. This verdict is also of importance as showing that the parochial system was in force in the land of Carlisle before the Red King incorporated it into the English kingdom. Other documents might be cited, supporting, if genuine, the title of the bishops of Durham to jurisdiction in the land of Carlisle. The title was good enough to sustain in the year 1255 a right to the profits of the benefices belonging to the bishopric of Carlisle *sede vacante* by the death, in that year, of Sylvester de Everdon, fifth bishop of Carlisle. Robert de Insula, bishop of Durham, also enforced a similar claim on the death of Robert de Chauncy, seventh Bishop of Carlisle.[1]

According to Fordun, in the Scotichronicon, the Bishop of Glasgow exercised jurisdiction in the land of Carlisle before Henry I. created the see of that name. He says:—

"Hic Henricus . . . videns Johannem Episcopum Glasguensem per Cumberlandiam ecclesias dedicare et cetera officia pontificalia secundum morem juris antiqui perficere cum nec sibi nec Archiepiscopo Eboracensi vellet inde ut domino et prelato obsecundare; incitante Turstino Eboracensi Archiepiscopo, constituit per vim et violentiam Eadwaldum Episcopum in Cumberlandia ad titulum Carleolensem, contra eum, quia non erat qui ei resistere audebat."

The Bishop of Glasgow, by way of protest against the dismemberment of his see, resigned his bishopric and retired into a monastery, but was afterwards recalled. The Bishops of Glasgow contined for long to maintain their claim, and in 1258, John de Cheham, bishop of Glasgow, spurred thereto by the allowance in 1255 of the claims of the Bishop of Durham upon the bishopric of Carlisle, went to Rome to urge his case there, but died on the road. The chronicle of Lanercost says:—

"obtendebat jus antiquum in partes Westmorlandiæ in prejudiciam Karleolensis ecclesiæ, dicens usque ad Rer Cross in Staymor ad diæcesem suam pertinere."

---

[1] "Letters from Northern Registers," p. 75, edited by James Raine, Canon of York. London: Longman & Co., 1873. Also Nicolson and Burn's "History of Westmorland and Cumberland," vol. ii. p. 257.

The Rey cross on Stainmoor was the most southern boundary in the sixth century of the see of Glasgow, which was then co-extensive with the kingdom of Strathclyde.

William II. and Henry I. must have found a strong Celtic element in the land of Carlisle, particularly in the west thereof, and these people would look to Glasgow and not to Durham for episcopal administrations, although the bishops of Glasgow had from the middle of the eleventh century resorted to York for consecration.

We thus have two great sees with conflicting claims to ecclesiastical jurisdiction over the land of Carlisle, when William II. incorporated it into the English kingdom, while Durham was in possession of, probably, the greater part of it. One or two minor claims have to be dealt with. A separate bishopric of Hexham existed from 681 to 820; the reasons for this division of the see of Lindisfarne into Lindisfarne and Hexham must be looked for in the histories of the sees of Durham and of York; the see of Hexham came to an end in 820. This see extended from the Tees to the Aln, and on the west extended as far as the river Eden at Wetheral; it no doubt advanced its borders from the boundary between Cumbria and Northumbria, under cover of Ecgfrid's conquest of Cumbria. This addition included, and was probably co-extensive with, the great estates which afterwards belonged to Gilles, the son of Bueth, and which became the barony of Gillesland, and the rural deanery of that name, whose existence it would otherwise be a puzzle to account for; it probably formed at a very early date the estate of some great thane, whose residence was at the mote of Irthington. On the see of Hexham the see of York had claims, arising out of the history of its formation.

We have mentioned the church of Candida Casa, Whithern, as the mother church of the district,[1] and St. Ninian as its bishop. He was not immediately succeeded by any bishop of Candida Casa, but at a later period an Anglian succession of bishops existed there, 732 to 803, and the line was revived again in the twelfth century. These bishops had no jurisdiction in the land of Carlisle, though we do find the bishops of the revived line acting in the north of England as episcopal curates or assistant bishops.

The Bishop of Durham in 1092 was William de S. Carilef, an unscrupulous Norman, who at first betrayed the interests of his king in favour of Odo of Bayeux, and then betrayed the interests of Odo of Bayeux in favour of his king, to whom he thus became reconciled. He issued a manifesto or charter, probably in 1092 or soon afterwards, by which he claimed Carlisle and all the surrounding country as being in his diocese; he died in 1096, and William II. kept the see vacant for three years and a half, when he appointed another Norman, Ralf, surnamed the Flambard, or the burning torch, an unprincipled minister, who suited well an unprincipled monarch. Ralf was consecrated in 1099; in the following year his patron was killed in the

---

[1] *Ante, p.* 23.

New Forest, and the new king, Henry I., clapped Ralf a prisoner into the Tower, from whence he escaped to the Continent. During his absence Henry I. severed the land of Carlisle, Hexhamshire, and Teviotdale from his diocese of Durham. Hexhamshire, which is not the same as the see of Hexham, and the land of Carlisle, he handed over to the see of York, then held by Archbishop Thomas II., while Teviotdale fell to the see of Glasgow.

The land of Carlisle was, in 1092, in a very disorganised condition, and in the wilder parts the inhabitants were, in the eyes of the adherents of the Roman use, little better than uncivilised heathen and heretics. Any religious houses that had existed in it, either at Carlisle or at Dacor, or just without it at St. Bees, had perished in the catastrophe of 876, and no religious house was, in 1092, existing in the land of Carlisle. This want the Norman rulers set themselves to supply, not perhaps so much from religious motives as from political reasons ; such houses were really missionary colonies, centres of civilisation as well as of religious life. The county histories and Dugdale print a charter by William II. under date of 1089, by which he founded a nunnery at Armathwaite, on the river Eden ; but this charter is a palpable forgery. We get on safer ground when we come to Walter, a wealthy Norman, whom the Red King left at Carlisle as master of the works ; he commenced to build a church there in honour of the Virgin Mary, and intended to found a religious house. On his death the work was taken up by Henry I., who, at the intercession of his queen, Matilda, founded in

1102 a house of Augustinian canons at Carlisle, and appointed his chaplain, Adulf, Athelwulf, or Æthelwulf, prior thereof. His name proves him to have been an Englishman, and he was prior of St. Oswald's, at Nostell in Yorkshire, also an Augustinian house. The church of the house was, from the first, a divided church; that is to say, the chancel belonged to the canons, the nave to the parishioners of St. Mary's parish, which was probably first constituted when Carlisle was re-founded by the Red King. Ranulph de Meschines gave his manor of Wetheral to Stephen, the abbot, and to the abbey of St. Mary's, of York, as an endowment for a Benedictine cell there. The charter, as printed in Dugdale, purports to be *pro anima Domini mei Regis Henrici*, but the MS. transcripts in the Harleian collection and in the library of the Dean and Chapter of Carlisle read: *Regis Willielmi*. What is called the original register was, in the last century, in the possession of the Dean and Chapter of Carlisle, but is now missing. Its production would hardly settle the question as to whether the cell of Wetheral was founded in the reign of William II. or Henry I., as it is itself but a copy, though of high authority and antiquity, of the original charters.

We have already, in writing of the claims of the see of Glasgow, a little anticipated matters, and mentioned that Henry I. constituted the land of Carlisle into the bishopric of Carlisle, and appointed Æthelwald or Æthelwulf the first bishop.

"*Anno* MCXXXIII. *mense Augusto, ante Assumptionem Sanctæ Mariæ apud Eboracum, a Thurstino Archiepiscopo consecrati sunt Episcopus Galfridus Cancellarius Regis Henrici ad Episcopatum Dunelmensem, Aldulfus Prior de Nostla ad urbem Karleol, quam Rex Henricus initiavit ad sedem Episcopalem datis sibi Ecclesiis de Cumberland et Westmorland, quæ adjacuerunt archidiaconatui Eboracensi."*—From Jo. HAGUST.

Another account says :—

"Fecit Rex Henricus novum Episcopatum apud Kardail in finibus Angliæ et Scotiæ, et posuit ibi Episcopum Adulfum, Priorem canonicorum regularium Sancti Oswaldi, cui solitus erat confiteri peccata sua : hic autem canonicos regulares posuit in ecclesia sua.—ANN. WAVERL.

Both of these accounts mention the new bishop as Prior of St. Oswalds, and not as Prior of Carlisle : this raises some doubt as to whether the first Prior and the first Bishop of Carlisle were one and the same person ; if so, he must have held high office in the Church, first prior and then bishop, from 1102 to 1156, the date of the death of the first bishop. As his name shows, Æthelwulf, the first bishop appointed to the Norman bishopric of Carlisle was an Englishman : there are two charters by this bishop in the register of Wetheral, dated probably immediately after his consecration, by which he confirms the churches of St. Michael and St. Lawrence at Appleby, of Kirkby Stephen, of Ormeshead, of Morland, of Clibburn, of Bromfield, and of Croglin, the cell of Wetheral with the parish of Warwick and the hermitage of St. Andrew to the monks of St. Mary's Abbey of York. He and his archdeacons, Elias and Robert, also confirmed the church of Crossby Ravensworth to the Abbey of Whitby in Yorkshire.

Little is known about Æthelwulf's doings. From

1136 his diocese, the land of Carlisle, was in the hands of the Scottish king, David, held as a fief of England by the heir to the Scottish throne. It was so held in the reign of Stephen until it was given up to Henry II. in 1157. Until 1138 Æthelwulf does not appear to have been able to obtain complete possession of his diocese, but in that year after the defeat of David, at the Battle of the Standard, Æthelwulf accompanied the legate, Alberic, to a provincial council of Scottish bishops at Carlisle: he was then admitted to possession of his see. In 1150 he was the first witness to the charter by which Prince Henry Fitz-David founded the Cistercian house of Holm Cultram in the west of his see: and he also witnessed the confirmation thereof by King David; the other witnesses are Walter, prior of Carlisle, and several persons bearing local names. This proves that Æthelwulf was in peaceful possession of his diocese with full consent of King David, and that it had not relapsed to Glasgow. The fact that in 1147 Æthelwulf supported Murdac as archbishop of York against Stephen's protégé, St. William of York, indicates that he had thrown his lot in with the Scottish king. He died in 1156. His diocesan machinery appears to have been complete. His first archdeacon was named Elias,[1] and his second Robert, and the archdeaconry was conterminous with the diocese. The parochial system was well developed and established. In the Augustinian house at Carlisle, the Benedictine

---

[1] Cartulary of Whitby, Surtees Society, vol. lxix. pp. 38, 260.

at Wetheral, and the Cistercian at Holm Cultram, he had the assistance of centres of missionary colonisation and civilisation planted in a somewhat wild district; synodals and ancient archidiaconal dues are mentioned in one of his charters.

Bernard, the second bishop of Carlisle, is a somewhat shadowy personage; his very existence has been doubted, and it has been stated that the see remained vacant from the death of Æthelwulf up to 1219. Bernard, however, was a real personage: bishop from 1156 to his death in 1186, and charters by him are in the registers of Lanercost and of Wetheral. The county histories state that he consecrated Lanercost in 1169; but his name does not appear in the list of witnesses to the foundation deed, while that of Christian, bishop of Candida Casa, does. This Christian was consecrated bishop of Candida Casa at Bermondsey, by the Archbishop of Rouen, acting for the Archbishop of York. His name appears frequently in the register of Holm; he acted as assistant-bishop in the northern dioceses, and in this capacity probably consecrated Lanercost Priory. After Bernard's death the king offered the see to Paulinus de Ledes, who refused it, though the king proposed to augment the income. For the next two years its revenues are accounted for by the sheriff in the Pipe Rolls; they only amount to £50. 19s. 6d. for that period, of which only 50s. reached the Treasury. The bishopric was not endowed with any landed property, but had the impropriation of the benefices of Carlton and Dalston in Cumberland, and Meaburn in Westmorland, and an annual payment of one mark from the school of Carlisle. The remainder of the income was made up from ecclesiastical dues. During the vacancy of the see the revenues and custody thereof were entrusted, as occasions arose, to the archdeacon for the time being, to Bernard, archbishop of Ragusa in 1203, and in 1215 to the Prior of Carlisle. Great confusion has been occasioned by there being two Bernards, and by Bernard, archbishop of Ragusa, being also called Archbishop of Sclavonia. There are two charters in the chartulary of Whitby, by Bernard, bishop of Carlisle, relating to the Church of Crossby Ravensworth, in Westmorland, which, from the witnesses to them, must belong to this second Bernard.

During this period of vacancy of the see, Carlisle and the district suffered severely from invasions by the Scotch. In 1173 and 1174 William the Lion invaded the district and besieged Carlisle. In 1216 Carlisle was again besieged and taken by Alexander of Scotland. Henry III. writes to Pope Honorius III. that Carlisle has revolted to the Scotch, and that the canons of Carlisle

"*in præjudicium juris nostri et Ecclesiæ Eboracensis ad instanciam Regis Scotiæ inimici nostri, quendam clericum suum interdictum et excommunicatum elegerunt sibi in Episcopum et pastorem,*"

and requests the pope to provide for the see. Accordingly, in 1218, the legate Gualio sends the canons of Carlisle into exile,—

"*eo quod regi Scottorum excommunicato, metu mortis coacti celebraverunt divina*" (CHRON. LANERCOST).

Gualio also appointed to the bishopric Hugh, abbot of Beaulieu (Bello Loco), in Burgundy, and committed the possessions of the canons to him. He was consecrated by the Archbishop of York, February 24, 1219. His episcopate was a brief one, but he appears to have been a firm administrator and a redresser of injustice; his charters in the registers of Holm, Wetheral, Lanercost, and Whitby show that he took care to make the monastic impropriators of livings in his diocese provide for the wants of these livings, and he did not hesitate to make them disgorge. In two of his charters he uses the peculiar style of "*Hugo dei gratia Karleolensis ecclesiæ vocatus sacerdos*," instead of "*Hugo dei gratia Karleolensis episcopus.*" He must also have reconstituted and re-endowed the Augustinian house at Carlisle after its canons had been expelled by Gualio. We know very little of the history of this body up to this date. The county historians give the first three priors as Æthelwulf, Walter, and John, the two last of whom appear as parties or witnesses to charters in the local registers; so also does P. (probably Peter), *priore Augustino et Rogero Canonicis Karleolensibus* (Register of Wetheral), and G., prior of Carlisle (Register of Lanercost), while the Chronicle of Lanercost says that Henry de Mariscis became prior of Carlisle in 1214, probably a brother of Richard de Marisco, bishop of Durham. The county histories also state that up to this time the bishop and the convent held their emoluments in common, and that Bishop Hugh effected a division between them. This must to some extent be an error; the Pipe Rolls of 1187 and 1188 show that the bishopric had an independent, though inadequate, endowment; and the language of the Chronicle of Lanercost shows that the possessions of the canons were also independent. The bishop did, no doubt, effect a division of the property, for he restored to the reconstituted house of Carlisle only part of its old endowment, retaining for his see the manor of Linstock, and there the bishops of Carlisle long had their residence. Bishop Hugh died in 1223, and the writer of the Chronicle of Lanercost, who was probably a friar minorite of Carlisle, thus viciously records the event:—

"*Hugo Carliolensis episcopus, qui conventum ejus ecclesiæ horribiliter dispersit et eorum possessiones fraudulenta divisione dimidiavit, justo Dei judicio, rediens a curia Romana, apud abbatiam quæ Forte dicitur, in partibus Burgundiæ, ingurgitatus, absque viatico et miserabiliter discessit die dominica infra octavas Ascensionis.*"

Bishop Hugh was at York, in 1220, when Henry III. of England and Alexander II. of Scotland met there and signed a truce, for the observance of which the bishop was one of the sureties. Whether he was one of the negotiators of the treaty or not does not appear; but from the very earliest establishment of the see of Carlisle up to the union of the kingdoms, to attend to Scottish affairs and truces, was part of the duties imposed upon the bishops of Carlisle.

Æthelwulf, the first bishop, was probably a courtier: the Bernards were shadows, and Hugh an administrative reformer; the fourth bishop, Walter Malclerk, was a diplomatist, and had represented, as ambassador or agent, the interests of King John at the

Papal Court during his contest with the barons. According to the Chronicle of Lanercost he was, at the time of his appointment, a canon of Carlisle, and he was also sheriff of Cumberland from the second year of Henry III. to the sixteenth, an office which he frequently exercised by deputy. During the twenty-three years that he held his see he devoted himself to a political life, and underwent the vicissitudes which politicians commonly undergo; in 1232 he was appointed by Henry III. Treasurer of the Exchequer, but was dismissed from office in the following year, with most of his colleagues, to make way for Poitevins, and other strangers. Bishop Walter was afterwards again in high favour, and employed as a diplomatist. He was catechist to Prince Edward, which is a curious appointment to be held by one who is said to have owed his name of Maleclerk to his scant stock of learning; he was also one of the lord justices when Henry III. went abroad in 1243. He was probably so taken up with the affairs of the state, as to have little time to attend to those of his diocese; considering the length of time he held office, his name rarely appears in the local chartularies. But he was able to attend to his own interests; probably by his influence his nephew, Radulf Barri, was appointed prior of Carlisle, on the death of Bartholomew, in 1231. He obtained, in 1230, from Henry III. a grant of the manor of Dalston, a manor in the forest of Cumberland, lying between the river Caldew and the Roman road from Carlisle to the west, which had escheated to the Crown in the reign of Henry II. The conveyance makes no mention of La Rose, or Rose Castle, or of any manor house, and probably there was none. The sheriff of Cumberland, who collected the profits, would not require a manor house either to reside in or for the reception of the profits, as Carlisle was a more convenient place. It may be observed that none of the manors in charge of the sheriff of Cumberland, as escheats, had manor houses. This grant brought the bishops of Carlisle into litigation, in which they were ultimately successful. In addition to thus securing a lasting and permanent benefit to his see, Bishop Walter Malclerk had, in 1244, a very valuable piece of picking granted to him, namely, the wardship of Walter Fitz Odard de Wigton, a babe of tender age, the owner of five fat manors within the see of Carlisle. This bishop was a great patron of the Friar Preachers, and it was under his patronage that, in 1233, the Friar Preachers, or Black Friars, and the Friar Minorites, or Grey Friars, settled in Carlisle, in localities which still retain their name. The Carmelites, or White Friars, had also a house at Appleby, and the Austin Friars, or Friars Eremite, one at Penrith. In a diocese like Carlisle, which must have required strenuous missionary efforts, the assistance of these friars must have been of the utmost value in spreading true Christianity; they soon acquired great popularity, and in the next century the *quatuor ordines* received many legacies from inhabitants of the see.

Bishop Walter Malclerk resigned his see in 1246, joined the Friar Preachers at Oxford, and died there in 1248.

Sylvester de Everdon, archdeacon of Chester, his successor in the see, was again a bishop of another type, a man of parchment, a lawyer, a clerk in the Chancery, who acquired, by practice in the engrossing of writs and deeds, a knowledge of law, which made him first vice-chancellor, and then, in 1244, chancellor of England, an office which he resigned in 1246, on his appointment as Bishop of Carlisle, wishing to devote himself to the affairs of his see; but he continued to take a leading part in the political and religious movements of the day, and was one of four prelates (viz., Canterbury, Winchester, Salisbury, and Carlisle) who, in 1253, called upon Henry III. as a deputation to remonstrate with him on his frequent violations of their privileges, the oppressions with which he had loaded them, and all his subjects, and the uncanonical, and forced elections which were made to vacant dignities. The king, in words of biting sarcasm, turned the tables on the prelates by suggesting that, as they had been thus elected, they had better resign :—

"*Et te, Sylvester Carleolensis, qui diu lambens cancellariam clericorum meorum clericulus extitisti, qualiter postpositis multis theologis et personis reverendis te episcopatum sublegavi.*"

The remonstrances of the prelates had this effect, that in 1255 the king ratified the great charter in most solemn manner, and the said prelates, with several others in equally solemn form, cursed all breakers of charters. In that same year Bishop Sylvester fell from his horse and broke his neck. He was more than once engaged in litigation for the protection of the rights of his see.

A bishop of another type now comes on the scene, a type of which many instances will appear, the local man. Thomas de Vipont, or Veteripont, member of a well-known local family, and rector of Graystock, a church in the diocese, succeeded Sylvester de Everdon, but he merely walks across the scene. Elected November, 1255, consecrated, in company with Henry, bishop of Candida Casa at St. Agatha's, Richmond, in Yorkshire, on February 7, 1255-6, he died in October, 1256. There is a solitary charter by him in the register of Holm Cultram, but his episcopate is memorable for the successful claim made by the Bishop of Durham to the profits of the benefices belonging to the bishopric of Carlisle, *sede vacante*.

The next bishop was Robert de Chauncy, or Chauncey: his name has been made into Chause and into de Chalize; but he was of the family of Chauncy de Chauncy, near Amiens, and afterwards of Scirpenbeck, near Pocklington, in Yorkshire. The name appears in documents in the chartulary of Whitby as Chauncy. He was, when appointed to Carlisle, archdeacon of Bath. He was brought up to medicine, and was physician to Eleanor, queen of Henry III., who presented him to a church worth 100 marks per annum. He was sheriff of Cumberland for a year and a half at the end of the reign of Henry III., and brought two Yorkshiremen, Robert and Roger de Pockington, to act as his deputies. Machel says he was sheriff for the first two years of Edward I., but this is doubtful. Richard de Crepping was sheriff at the accession of Edward I., having succeeded the bishop shortly before the death of the old king. There was evidently a quarrel between the two, for the sheriff, in the first year of Edward I., informed the Lord Chancellor that the bishop had forbidden his tenants to take the oath of fealty to the new monarch, who was then abroad; this the prelate denied, saying the sheriff was at fault in not having attended to receive their fealty. The bishop, shortly after this, excommunicated the sheriff for levying an illegal distress on the convent of Holm Cultram, but a writ of prohibition compelled the bishop to retract. Bishop Chauncy appears to have played no part in the great political struggles of the reign of Henry III. That doubt should be cast upon the readiness of his tenants to pay fealty to Edward I. may indicate that his sympathies were liberal. During the episcopate of this bishop much litigation took place about the church of Crosby Ravensworth, in the diocese of Carlisle, which the abbey of Whitby held under various charters and archiepiscopal and episcopal confirmations. An account of the proceedings is in the chartulary of Whitby, published by the Surtees Society. The result is not known, but these proceedings, and the charters of Crosby Ravensworth, introduce several officials of the diocese of Carlisle, whose names we do not remember to have seen in the local chartularies, such as the official of the Archdeacon of Carlisle, and the *magister stolarum* there. The officials, both of the bishop and the archdeacon, held their courts in the cathedral of Carlisle, as did special judges appointed by the pope, an appointment held by this bishop at Carlisle, before he was appointed to the see.

The Chronicle of Lanercost sums up the character of this bishop thus:—

"*Divini honoris fervidus, amator humanitatis, et urbanitatis promptus executor, qui quam dapsilis et largus extiterit sine nobis mundus attestari poterit.*"

On the 13th of December, 1278, the canons of Carlisle elected as bishop William de Rothelfeld, dean of York; all the formalities were carried out to complete the election, but de Rothelfeld refused to accept the office. On this the chapter, without waiting for a second *congé d'élire*, nay, even after being inhibited by the king, proceeded to a second election and chose Ralph de Irton, a member of a Cumberland family, who was prior of Gisburne, in Yorkshire. For this the canons were attached, and made answer that they did not know they were doing wrong, and submitted themselves to the pleasure of the king, Edward I., but the bishop elect went off to Rome to urge his interests there. The pope, Nicholas III., appointed a commission to ascertain the facts; they reported that both elections were irregular, the canons having appointed a committee of their body, the prior, precentor, succentor, cellarius, and subsacrist, to elect: and that, owing to the death of the Archbishop of York difficulties had arisen as to the confirmation of the second election. The pope, by bull dated April, 1280, solved the difficulty in a highly diplomatic manner. He declared the election void as not made by all the electors, and then of his own authority appointed Ralph de Irton, bishop of Carlisle. The pope thus judiciously avoided offending the king by countenancing an election which the king had declared void; he judiciously avoided upholding the king's authority, for he declared the election void on different grounds to those on which the king had done so: and he also established a precedent for the pope appointing an English bishop. The king submitted as tamely to the pontiff as the prior and convent did to the king. The bishop returned to England on May 30, 1280, and, in September of that year, Edward I. and Eleanor, his queen, visited Lanercost and hunted in Inglewood Forest. In October of that year, Bishop Irton held a convocation of his clergy in his cathedral (*in ecclesia majori Karleolensi*), who granted him the tenths of the churches for two years, to be paid according to the *verum valorem*, and out of the new money within a year. The writer of the Chronicle of Lanercost says:—

"*Unde solvimus in universo viginti quatuer libras et. Unde de ista materia dixit H. sic—*

>*Grex desolatus, pastore diu viduatus,*
>*Sic cito tonderi non indiget, immo foveri :*
>*Grex desolatus, nimis hactenus extenuatus,*
>*Jam confortari debet, non excoriari.*
>*Sed si pastor oves habeat tondere necesse,*
>*Debet ei pietas, modus, et moderamen inesse.*"

In 1281 this bishop brought to a successful conclusion the litigation about the manor and advowson of Dalston, which had arisen out of the grant thereof to Bishop Sylvester de Everdon. The king, Bishop Irton, the prior and convent of Carlisle, and the parson of Thursby, were all parties to further litigation about the tithes of Linethwaite and Curthwaite, which places were assarts or enclosures in the forest of Inglewood in the parish of Aspatria: the king was decided to have the best title, and he shortly granted them to the prior and convent of Carlisle. This is important as showing that civilisation was advancing in the diocese, and these assarts ultimately became parishes carved out of the extensive parish of Aspatria. Spite of the method of his appointment, Bishop Irton enjoyed the confidence of Edward I., and was employed in many important and confidential missions, particularly in connexion with Scotland and the claims thereto advanced by Edward I. He died at his palace at Linstock, near Carlisle, on March 1, 1292, from the effects of fatigue occasioned by a winter journey from London. The Chronicle of Lanercost describes him as—

"*Vir callidus et providus sed admodum cupidus, qui visitationes ecclesiarum vertit in voraginem quæstuum et ad fabricam culminis majoris ecclesiæ suæ sedis extorsit per totam diœcesem a simplicibus sacerdotibus anniversariis muletam inhonestam.*"

CHAPTER VI.

THE SCOTTISH WARS.

THE new Bishop of Carlisle was chosen from the canons of that place. John de Halucton, de Haloghton (his name is variously spelt, but he is best known as John Halton), was elected on St. George's Day (April 23rd), 1292. In the following month, on the Sunday within the octave of the Ascension, a dire misfortune befell his cathedral and cathedral city; a tremendous hurricane, evidently from the west, blew for twenty-four hours, parching up the vegetation, forcing men and horses off their roads, and driving the sea up higher, no doubt over Burgh and Rockcliff marshes, than ever had been known before, to the destruction of large numbers of cattle and sheep. In the midst of this terrible storm, an incendiary set fire to his father's house, which was just outside the city walls, near the west end of the cathedral: the flames spread, and the whole city and suburbs were destroyed with the exception of a few houses and the church of the Black Friars. The Chronicle of Lanercost preserves the following:—

> "VERSUS DE COMBUSTIONE KARLIOLI.
> "Pro dolor immensis, Maii sub tempore mensis,
> Ignibus accensis, urbs arsit Karliolensis;
> Urbs desolata, cujus sunt aspera fata,
> Flammis vastata, misere jactet incinerata.
> Ecce, repentinis datur inclyta villa ruinis,
> Fitque cremata cinis, salvis tantum Jacobinis.[1]

---
[1] The French name for the Black Friars.

> Organa, campanæ, vox musica canonicorum,
> Jam menti sanæ sunt instrumenta dolorum.
> Post desolamen urbs sentiat hæc relevamen,
> Fiat, fiat Amen; hoc audi, Christe, precamen."

From the special mention of them, we may conclude the organs and bells in the cathedral had been such as the canons might be proud of. In this fire the muniments of the city and the see perished. Charters granted at a later date to the city of Carlisle recite the destruction in this fire of all earlier ones: the earliest existing register of the bishops of Carlisle commences in 1292, shortly after this fire. This register and its successors record the acts of Bishops Halton, Ross, Kirkby, Welton, and Appleby, from 1292 to 1396, a period nearly coinciding with the Scottish wars of Edward I., II., and III., in which Carlisle as a fortress was of the highest importance, while its bishops filled high military and political offices, often being captains and governors of Carlisle, and always lords marchers. All the transactions of the diocese which were conducted in writing are recorded in the registers of the five bishops we have mentioned. Other entries of wider interest relating to diocesan, national, and even international politics occur at intervals. More than one hundred most interesting wills, mainly of persons of the upper-middle class are transcribed in these volumes, which also contain very full lists of ordinations. These volumes have recently been transcribed at the expense of the Cumberland and Westmorland Antiquarian and Archæological Society, and are in slow course of being edited for the press.

In the year of Halton's accession to the episcopate, 1292, the new and stringent valuation of church property known as the Taxation of Pope Nicholas was made, in order to facilitate the collection of a tenth of all ecclesiastical property which Edward I. had obtained from that pope on taking a new vow of crusade. This *Taxatio* was known as the *Verus* or *Novus Valor*, by way of distinction from one made in 1253, the *Vetus Valor*, under a grant by Innocent III. to Henry III. of first fruits and tenths. The *Taxatio* of Pope Nicholas remained in general force until the *Valor Ecclesiasticus* of Henry VIII., but it was, for a portion of the province of York, superseded by the *Nova Taxatio* of 1318, to which we shall presently come. We give a condensed summary of the valuation for the diocese of Carlisle :—

SPIRITUALITIES.

Deanery of Carlisle	£711	2	4
Deanery of Allerdale	503	14	0
Deanery of Westmorland	788	10	8
Deanery of Cumberland	544	2	10
The Archdeacon's synodals, &c.	10	0	0
	£2,557	9	10
Temporalities	613	15	9½
	£3,171	5	7½

Three parishes in the deanery of Carlisle, and one in the deanery of Westmorland, are exempt as not exceeding ten marks in annual value.

Bishop Halton was appointed to collect from the Scottish bishops and clergy their tenths under the Taxation of Pope Nicholas; he had as coadjutor the Bishop of Caithness, and he employed a large staff of the Scottish regular clergy as sub-collectors; but frequent entries in his register prove that the collection was a work of time and difficulty, and the terrors of excommunication had often to be had resource to. Lists of the sums collected are preserved in the register; this business frequently took Bishop Halton into Scotland, and many of his writs and orders for regulation of his own diocese are dated from Jedburgh.

Bishop Halton succeeded his predecessor Bishop Irton as one of the commissioners appointed for trial of the merits of the many claims made to the Crown of Scotland. He was present at Berwick in October and November, 1292, when judgment was given in favour of John Balliol, to whom the Scottish castles were at once given up. Difficulties soon arose, and in 1294 Bishop Halton went to Scotland as ambassador from Edward I. under letters of safe-conduct from John Balliol; but Balliol and the Scottish barons could not endure their position as vassals, and entered into an alliance with France. In 1296 war between England and Scotland was precipitated by the refusal of Balliol to attend a parliament at Newcastle, the massacre of a small body of English troops, and the investment of Carlisle by the Scots, under the Earl of Buchan, who, finding Carlisle too strong for him, and the citizens too determined,—the very women taking part in the fighting,—raided through the district and committed horrible atrocities, sparing neither man, woman, nor child, and falling upon the religious houses at

Lambley, Lanercost, and Hexham. The first, a small nunnery on the borders of Cumberland and Northumberland, they utterly destroyed; at Lanercost they burned the conventual buildings, but the church escaped, owing probably to a report that the English king, with an army, was approaching; on this the Earl of Buchan retired into Scotland. Edward I. destroyed Berwick. Balliol, by a formal instrument, copy whereof in Halton's register, renounced the homage he had paid to the English king, who took possession of Scotland, and filled all the important posts with Englishmen. Scotland rose in 1297 under Wallace, who, in that year, after his victory at Stirling, again harried Lanercost, and summoned Carlisle to surrender, but withdrew on finding the garrison prepared for defence. During this year Robert Bruce swore fealty to Edward I. on the sword of St. Thomas before Bishop Halton, one of a series of historical pageants that about this time were held in Carlisle cathedral, and which might well supply scenes for the painter's brush. In the following year, 1298, Edward I., after the battle of Falkirk, was compelled to retire with his victorious army upon Carlisle, where entries in the bishop's register show that large stores were being accumulated in the castle of which Bishop Halton was now the *custos*. The register contains very interesting accounts, both originals and copies from the Exchequer Rolls, of expenses incurred by the bishop as such *custos*. It also contains petitions that allowances may be made to him for damage caused by the passage of troops to Scotland. The king shortly went south, but in 1299 he wrote to Bishop Halton that he would be at Carlisle by midsummer; he did not, however, come until the next year, 1300, when he was followed by his new Queen, Margaret.

At Carlisle he assembled one of the finest and most brilliant armies England had ever put in the field, and proceeded to Caerlaverock Castle, which he besieged and took, as also other fortresses in the south of Scotland; but the country was too impoverished to sustain his army, and he made a truce and withdrew. On this occasion he and his queen were the guests of the church at the abbeys of Holm Cultram and Lanercost and at the episcopal palace of Rose. At Holm Cultram the Bishop of Glasgow, then prisoner, swore allegiance under circumstances of great solemnity. Edward I. returned south, but the Scottish nobles and Wallace kept the war up until Wallace was captured and hanged in 1305. In 1306 Robert Bruce stabbed John Comyn of Badenoch, of the rival house of Balliol, in the church of the Greyfriars at Dumfries, and was shortly afterwards crowned King of Scotland at Scone. This roused the old king's ire; he sent his son on in advance, who ruthlessly wasted the Scottish country; the king followed in easy stages, and he and the queen arrived at Lanercost in September, 1306, and stayed there for six months, with the exception of a short visit to Carlisle and to Bishop Halton at Linstock. From Lanercost Edward I. summoned a Parliament to meet at Carlisle on January 20, 1306-7. The Prince of Wales, the Archbishop of York, nineteen bishops, thrice that number of mitred abbots, a large number of the most powerful barons of the realm, and the great officers of state, came to Carlisle to attend this Parliament, which passed the statute of Carlisle, forbidding the payment of talliages on monastic property, and other imposts by which money was raised to be sent out of the country. To Carlisle also came Cardinal Petrus Hispanus (Cardinal Peter d'Espagnol), the papal legate. He preached in the cathedral at Carlisle, and,—

"revested himselfe and the other bishops which were present, and then, with candels light and causing the bels to be roong, they accursed, in terrible wise, Robert Bruce, the vsurper of the crowne of Scotland, with all his partakers, aiders, and mainteiners."—*Holinshed*, ii. 523.

About midsummer another stately ceremony took place in Carlisle cathedral; the king made there solemn offering of the horse litter in which he had travelled to the north and of the horses belonging to it. On July 3 he mounted his charger and set off towards Scotland, but died on Burgh Marsh on July 7, 1307. Faint traditions of his funeral pageant passing over Staynmoor still linger there, and the splendours of the Parliament of Carlisle were not forgotten by the citizens three centuries later.

The heir to the throne arrived at Carlisle from Wales on July 18, and on the 20th was proclaimed king, and received homage at the castle from the English nobles, who were assembled for the Scottish expedition. He accompanied his father's funeral for a few days' march, and then returned to Carlisle and proceeded thence to Dumfries, where he received homage from some of the Scotch nobility, but he soon went to the South for his father's funeral. With the proclamation of Edward II. the most brilliant period of the history of Carlisle comes to a close. Its importance as a fortress was in no way diminished, but no great armies were again assembled under its walls for the conquest of Scotland; Berwick rather than Carlisle became their *rendezvous;* Bishop Halton continued to act on the royal behalf in Scottish matters, but the character of the war changed; the English were worsted, and his diocese was overrun and wasted. Large sums were wrung out of it for ransom, or hostages given in default of payment. In 1311 Robert Bruce was at Lanercost for three days; in 1314 Edward Bruce visited Rose for a like period, and laid the country waste throughout the forest of Inglewood, while the bishop was blockaded in Carlisle, which was too strong for Bruce. After Bannockburn, Gillesland was compelled to pay tribute and the inhabitants to swear allegiance to Bruce. In 1315 occurred the famous siege of Carlisle by Robert Bruce, and its gallant and successful defence by Andrew de Hercla; in 1322 Robert Bruce burnt Rose Castle, ravaged Holm Cultram Abbey, and twice in that year wasted the country far and wide. No wonder that the bishop was fugitive from his diocese; in 1318 he addressed a piteous letter to the pope, in which he states that he is reduced to indigence, and asks for the appropriation to his see of the living of Horncastle, in Lincolnshire, as a means of support. This he obtained, and Horncastle and other Lincolnshire livings belonged to the Bishop of Carlisle until the time of

Bishop Percy. The bishop writes from Melburn, in Derbyshire, a church which was also appropriated to his see. He died in November, 1324, at Rose Castle, says the Chronicle of Lanercost. He held an ordination in that year at Horncastle, under licence from his brother of Lincoln. His last public duty, other than the duties of his see, was as commissioner for peace with Scotland in 1320.

His residence in the beginning of his episcopate was at Linstock, where, in 1292, he entertained John Romanus, archbishop of York, who, with a large suite, was *en route* to his archiepiscopal peculiar of Hexham. In 1300 Edward I. and Queen Margaret stayed for a short time at Rose; in 1307 they were Bishop Halton's guests at Linstock. The bishop in that year was evidently anxious to obtain a new residence for his see, for he petitioned for ground within the city of Carlisle on which to build one. He probably planned, though he may not have carried out, Rose Castle, on the plan partly remaining until now,—namely, a concentric Edwardian castle: in this would be incorporated, as at Naworth, an older peel tower, which, with a lot of wooden buildings, probably accommodated Edward I. and his queen. There would be no better accommodation at Linstock.

So great was the devastation wrought by the Scots during the later part of this prelate's time, that in 1318 a royal mandate was issued to Bishop Halton to make a *Nova Taxatio* over part of the province of York, as the clergy were unable to pay the tax according to the *Valor* of Pope Nicholas. To give an instance of the difference: in the valuation of Pope Nicholas the temporalities of the Priory of Lanercost are set down as £74. 12s. 6½d. per annum; in the *Nova Taxatio* they are returned as nothing. The same return is made as to most of the churches on the borders of Cumberland. This was not a new condition of things in 1318. So early as 1302 Bishop Halton had to direct the collectors of the disme, or tenth, to collect nothing from certain churches, those along the border, and two-thirds only from a long list of other churches.

Strange and marked must have been the contrast between the splendour and plenty in Carlisle during the visits of Edward I. and the poverty in the country around; the citizens of Carlisle waxing fat on the wages of the soldiery, while the wretched peasants around them starved.

The canons of Carlisle, on January 7, 1325, elected William de Armyne, who, as rector of Levington, had been, in 1314, proctor in Parliament for Bishop Halton, and who now, as canon of York, was *custos sede vacante* of the spiritualities and temporalities of the see, but John Ross, a man from the south (*homo australis*, the chronicler of Lanercost contemptuously calls him) was consecrated bishop by the pope. The Chronicle makes no further mention of him except that he died at Rose in 1334, an error for 1332, *et ad sepeliendum delatus est ad partes australes Angliæ*. That he officiated in 1327 at Westminster on the occasion of the consecration of a Bishop of Candida Casa; that he found his diocese in dire poverty, without even a manor house, he says, capable of covering him and his *familia*, that he was anxious about the appropriation of Horncastle; that he got into debt and into a tremendous litigation with the prior of Carlisle, whom he excommunicated, is about all we know of the "man from the south."

The following document is copied from the register of Bishop Ross, and is dated shortly after his consecration. The bishop appears to be obtaining from the treasury of his cathedral church a sufficient supply of vestments, plate, and service-books for his own private use; they had probably been returned to the treasury by the executors of his predecessor:—

"Indentura inter episcopum et capitulum Karl. de vestimentis et rebus infra scriptis.

"Hec indentura testatur quod venerabilis Pater J. miseratione divina et apostolice sedis gratia Karl. Episcopus ex accommodato recipit de subpriore et conventu ecclesie Karl. mortuo priore ejusdem per manus Walteri de Ebor, ejusdem ecclesie sacriste vestimenta et alia subscripta.

"Unam casulam rubeam de Samito cum tunica et dalmatica de sindone rubea ejusdem secte cumque alba cum parura de armis Regis et comitis Lincoln.

"Item j tunicam et dalmaticam de sindone rubea pro Diacono et Subdiacono.

"Item j casulam cum tunica et dalmatica de baudekyn unius secte cum alba stola manipulo et pertinenciis de serico consutis.

"Item alias duas albas cum pertinenciis pro diacono et subdiacono.

"Item unam casulam cotidianam.

"Item unam cappam de samito rubeo cum morsura.

"Item duas cappas crocei coloris.

"Item duo pallia altaris cum parura brodata et tercium sine parura.

"Item j Baudekyn integrum pro frontelio.

"Item j missale sine Evangeliis et Epistolis.

"Item j Alium librum Evangeliorum et Epistolarum.

"Item j Pontificale.

"Item duo Gradualia.

"Item unum calicem argenteum deauratum.

"Item duo Fiala argentea.

"Item unum Baculum pestoralem cum capite de argento et deaurato.

"Item unam Mitram gemmatam et unam aliam simplicem.

"Item unam par cirothecarum cum uno annulo pontificali.

"Item unum Thuribulum argenteum et deauratum.

"Item unum superaltare.

"Item unum crismatorium argenteum.

"Item unum parvum librum pro confirmatione puerorum cum una Stola et ij. cofris.

"Data Karl. die Dominica proxima post festum Translacionis Sancti Thome Martiris Anno gracie ut supra."

Bishop Ross was succeeded by John de Kirkby, a canon of Carlisle, a new type of bishop, for he was churchman, diplomatist and soldier. As a soldier he was no mere *custos* of Carlisle, acting on the defensive, organising troops and collecting provisions and stores: he himself headed the troops, and fought in person. He does not appear to have accompanied, in 1334, the forces which assembled at Carlisle under Edward Balliol and invaded Scotland, or those which Edward III. collected there in the following year. But, in 1337, he and some of the local barons invaded Scotland with a force raised in Cumberland and Westmorland, and effected a junction with an English army under the Earl of Warwick, which had entered Scotland by Berwick. The united forces did much mischief in Scotland, and Bishop Kirkby became especially obnoxious to the Scots, who in his absence raided into Cumberland, burnt the hospital of St.

Nicholas, in the suburbs of Carlisle, and visited Rose, which they burnt and wasted. In the following year Bishop Kirkby and Ralph Dacre, lord of Gilsland, invaded Scotland and raised the siege of Edinburgh, then held by the English, and invested by a Scottish army. In 1345, the Scots under Sir William Douglas raided through Cumberland, and wasted Penrith and Gilsland. They were harassed by a small force under Bishop Kirkby and Sir Thomas Ogle, who fell in with a detached party of Scots under Sir Alexander Strachan. In the skirmish that ensued, Strachan was killed by Ogle, who was dangerously wounded. Bishop Kirkby was unhorsed, but recovered his saddle, rallied his men, and gained the victory.

These wars much impoverished the already poor see. In 1337 the bishop says he cannot collect the tenths, because the clergy had all fled; his register shows by various entries that much pressure was put upon him by the king to make him raise money and men-at-arms. To these demands the bishop declined to accede; indeed, he stood up manfully for his clergy, who declared that, so far from paying procurations, tenths, and other imposts, they could hardly live. The bishop positively refused to collect or even to acknowledge a grant of wool from the clergy, made by the Parliament of Nottingham. Poverty and misery were everywhere throughout the diocese. The priory of Lanercost, in 1346, was reduced for the future to utter insignificance by a savage and barbarous raid of the Scots, under David Bruce. Bishop Kirkby, spite of his pluck and fighting powers, was unable to maintain his position in his diocese: he was frequently absent on compulsion, and his ordinations were necessarily held at many places outside of his own diocese. Within it he does not seem to have been popular. At Penrith, in 1333, and at Caldewstanes, in the suburbs of Carlisle, in 1337, he and his suite were hooted, mobbed, stoned, and wounded by rioters. He was also engaged in a long and expensive litigation with his chapter and with his archdeacon. He died in 1352. During his episcopate, in 1349, the Black Death ravaged the province of York, but we have found no special mention of its ravages in the diocese of Carlisle. There is, however, a gap of about seven years in the episcopal registers at this time, from 1346 or thereabouts. This would seem to indicate that the administration of the diocese was in much confusion in the last years of Kirkby's episcopate; and it hinders any inquiry as to whether any unusual number of benefices were vacated about the time of the Black Death.

On this vacancy of the see, as on those occasioned by the deaths of Bishops Chauncey and Halton, disputes arose as to the succession, the Papal Court steadily continuing its policy of arrogating to itself the nomination to English archbishoprics and bishoprics and to the choicest pieces of ecclesiastical preferment. These it generally conferred on foreigners, and the unpopularity of such appointments had much to do with bringing about the Reformation. The impoverished diocese of Carlisle, however, offered slight attraction to Italian priests, who would require strong inducements to overcome their natural dislike to its climate. On the first of these vacancies just mentioned the Papal Court had, as we have seen, secured a diplomatic victory, and set a valuable precedent by declaring the election by the chapter void, and by itself appointing *auctoritate sua* the nominee of the chapter. In the second case the Papal Court improved upon the precedent, and put in its nominee, the *homo australis*, though the king had confirmed Wm. de Armyne, the nominee of the chapter. On the present occasion the Papal Court still further vindicated its authority; the chapter of Carlisle, under *congé d'élire*, elected their prior, John de Horncastle, as bishop of Carlisle, and he was confirmed therein by the king. In the Carlisle episcopal registers a page is headed, *Registrum Dni Johannis de Horncastro Electi et Confirmati, &c.*, and he had restitution of the temporalities. A writ addressed to him by the king, and two nominations by him to benefices, are recorded in the registers. John de Horncastle was *de facto* bishop of Carlisle from February, 1352, to February, 1353, when he had to make place for the papal nominee, Gilbert de Welton, by his name possibly a local man. Bishop Welton died in 1362, and the canons of Carlisle, under *congé d'élire*, elected one of their own body, Thomas de Appleby. The pope declared the election void, but *auctoritate sua* appointed de Appleby to the see. He held the see until 1395.

There is no necessity to linger over Bishops Welton and Appleby; they were both associated with the local magnates in many commissions, of which we need not give a list, for regulating Scottish matters;

and to that extent they were political personages, important political personages, but their registers contain no documents equal in historical interest to those in the registers of Halton, Ross, and Kirkby. The Scottish wars were dying down, though Carlisle was unsuccessfully attacked by the Scots in 1385 and 1387: Richard II. was too feeble a monarch to make himself much felt in the far North: thus the history of the diocese of Carlisle ceases to mingle so much as before with the general history of England. These registers contain a great mass of matter of local interest, both to the genealogist and to the topographer, and it is to be hoped that they will be shortly made accessible in print. They throw much light on the architectural history of the cathedral and other churches, while the wills, already mentioned, which belong wholly to the second half of the fourteenth century, are of the deepest interest from the glimpses they give into social life at that time. An unusual proportion of these wills are of clergy beneficed in the diocese; a perusal of them shows that the reverend testators were by no means badly off, their wills dealing with both real and personal property. Several of them farmed to a considerable extent, to judge from the horses and cattle they had to dispose of, while bequests of clothes, beds, hangings, brass pots, brewing utensils, and the like indicate that some of the beneficed clergy, poor as the diocese was, were well clad and dwelt in well-furnished residences. Bequests of books occur, mainly of service books, but occasionally of others. Thomas de Byx leaves books to the library of the prior and convent of Carlisle, *unum par Clementinarum et unum Decretalium*. From the wills of both clerics and laics we gather that the *quatuor ordines* of friars in the diocese were popular; bequests to them of money are frequent, and their churches were favourite places of interment. Provision is made for much feasting at funerals, and all poor and all clerks who attended generally received a meal and a fee. The fabric fund of the cathedral frequently receives bequests, and so do the bridges at Carlisle, Appleby, Salkeld, and Kirkbythore: for these bridges and for the cathedral money was frequently raised by indulgences. William de Routhbury, archdeacon of Carlisle, leaves 40s. for the repairs of the chancel roof and window of Great Salkeld church, but if his successor, the new archdeacon, makes any claim for dilapidations he revokes the bequest. The ordination lists preserved in the registers show that the number of clergy in the diocese must have been very large in proportion to the number of the laity, and far beyond the number for which benefices could be found; judging from their names the persons ordained came, as a rule, from the lower orders of society, and were mainly natives of the diocese.

Either Bishop Welton or Appleby provided the diocese with a new set of "Constitutions": a copy is in the volume containing Welton's and Appleby's registers, bound up between the two. They occupy a considerable space, and are too long for reproduction here, containing some sixty chapters. Internal evidence shows that they were laid before a diocesan synod, by whom they were ratified, thus making them diocesan law. Each chapter is taken almost *verbatim* from one or another of the many similar compilations printed in the *Concilia* of Spelman and Wilkins, but the Bishop of Carlisle has not adopted any one code *en bloc*, though he greatly favours one drawn up by Peter Quivil, bishop of Exeter, 1287. The two last chapters, *De habitu clericorum et Indumentis* and *Nota de Perjuris et per quos absolvi*, have a strong local smack. By the first the clergy were prohibited from wearing cloaks with long sleeves (*capæ manicatæ*) or other garments of levity, but they were to wear *capæ clausæ*, or *superpellicia*, up to the feast of St. Peter ad Vincula, after which date they were to provide themselves with *capæ clausæ*, otherwise the offending garments were to be forfeited *fabricæ Pontis de Eden juxta Karl.* In the second the bishop laments the prevalence of perjury in the diocese of Carlisle, and directs that perjurers confessing their perjury are not to be absolved except *in periculo mortis*.

During the period covered by this and the preceding chapter we have little information about the prior and convent of Carlisle except that they were generally at loggerheads or litigation with their bishop, who was generally imposed upon them by Papal provision to the prejudice of the prior and convent's selection under a *congé d'élire*. This culminated in a grand riot when William de Dalston, elected prior about 1385, refused to profess canonical obedience to Bishop Appleby. The bishop directed the parish priest of St. Mary's in the cathedral to denounce the prior *inter sollempnia missarum* as excommunicate.

A riot ensued, and the priest was hustled out of the church. The archbishop intervened, and in the end the prior, who was also accused of immorality, had to resign his office. Contests at this time between bishops and their chapters were by no means peculiar to this diocese, the monastic bodies generally struggling for freedom from episcopal control.

The episcopal registers, 1292 to 1396, contain many instances of indulgences to raise money for the repair of the cathedral of Carlisle, which had suffered much by fire and at the hands of the Scots. Several indulgences for the same purpose were granted by the archbishops of York, and will be found in their registers: some of them are printed in the Surtees Society's publications, vol. xliv., Priory of Hexham.

CHAPTER VII.

A CENTURY AND A QUARTER OF BISHOPS.

ON the death of Bishop Appleby in 1395 the prior and convent of Carlisle procured a *congé d'élire* from the king, and elected Bishop William Strickland, or Stirkland, member of a well-known and ancient family in Westmorland. Again the Papal Court disregarded the chapter's election, and in 1396 imposed upon them Robert Reid, bishop of Dromore, and a Dominican friar, who was almost immediately translated to Chichester. He was, in 1397, succeeded by Thomas Merks, a monk of Westminster: who probably owed his elevation to the Papal Court. So far as local matters are concerned, he is a mere nonentity—no acts of his in his diocese are recorded; but to many he is the best known of the early bishops of Carlisle by reason of his speech on behalf of his king in Shakespeare's play of Richard the Second. Bishop Merks was the only person who raised his voice in Parliament to protest against the deposition of Richard II. :—

> " Worst in this royal presence may I speak,
> Yet best beseeming me to speak the truth.
> Would God, that any in this noble presence
> Were enough noble to be upright judge
> Of noble Richard; then true nobless would
> Learn him forbearance from so foul a wrong.

What subject can give sentence on his king?
And who sits here that is not Richard's subject?

* * * *

" And shall the figure of God's Majesty,—
His captain, steward, deputy elect,
Anointed, crowned, planted many years,—
Be judg'd by subject and inferior breath,
And he himself not present? O forbid it, God,
That, in a Christian climate, souls refined
Should show so heinous, black, obscene a deed!
I speak to subjects, and a subject speaks,
Stirr'd up by heaven thus boldly for his king."

* * * *

The EARL of NORTHUMBERLAND.
" Well have you argued, sir; and, for your pains
Of capital treason we arrest you here.
My lord of Westminster, be it your charge
To keep him safely till his day of trial."

The poet puts sentence on the bishop in the mouth of Bolingbroke (Henry IV.),—

" Carlisle, this is your doom:—
Choose out some secret place, some reverend room,
More than thou hast, and with it joy thy life,
So, as thou liv'st in peace, die free from strife;
For, though mine enemy thou hast ever been,
High sparks of honour in thee have I seen."

Merks was deprived of his bishopric, but allowed to accept other preferment, and died a Gloucestershire rector. He is the first Bishop of Carlisle of whom a portrait has come down to us; it represents him in the choir-tippet and hood of a monk of Westminster.

With the accession of Bishop Reid we lose the assistance we have had during the fourteenth century of the episcopal registers: no episcopal registers are in existence for the diocese of Carlisle from 1396 to 1561, unless by some miracle Bishop Strickland's register still survives; it was in the possession of Lord William Howard of Naworth in 1606, as is shown in a paper in the seventh volume of the "Transactions of the Cumberland and Westmorland Antiquarian and Archæological Society." Nothing exists to supply the place of these registers. Canon Raine, in the preface to "Letters from Northern Registers," says:—

"It is much to be regretted that, in a city like Carlisle, which is one of the gateways into Scotland, so few documentary memorials should have been preserved. Their destruction, however, was probably due to that restless people whose dangerous proximity has invested with such interest the past history of the capital of the Borders."

We hardly are inclined to put quite so much blame on our neighbours. The earlier records, ecclesiastical and civil, perished in the conflagration of 1292, none being left. The later perished in the time of the Troubles, between 1643 and 1649 or 1660, a few alone, like the two volumes of episcopal registers we have dealt with, the volume containing the episcopal acts from 1561 to 1643, and the Dormant Book of the city of Carlisle, luckily escaping. The monastic chartularies survived this second period of ruin, because they had gone as muniments of title into the hands of those who had got the property of the religious houses dissolved at the Reformation.

To Bishop Merks there succeeded in 1400, on petition of the king by papal provision, William

Strickland, the same whom the pope had in 1396 set aside: Henry IV. had purchased the support of the Church by the promise of persecution, and the Papal Court would accede readily to the king's wishes. The pledge of persecution was speedily redeemed: very strong powers were given to the bishops for the repression of heresy and of the wandering preachers, or Lollards, who had in the last years of the fourteenth century spread far and wide the doctrines of Wyclif. The infamous Statute of Heretics soon followed, bristling with terrible provisions, to be worked by the bishops, and for the first time placing on the statute book the penalty of death by fire for religious opinions. No evidence exists to connect Bishop Strickland with the enforcement of these measures in his diocese, nor is it known how far Lollardism had a hold there; that it had some is probable from the fact that John of Gaunt, an accredited protector thereof, was in Carlisle from 1380 to 1384 as the king's lieutenant on the Borders. The diocese also probably contained many sympathisers with Richard II., who would hold by the belief that the body exposed at Pontefract was not his, but that he was alive, well, and with the Scots. Such persons would be likely to aid the Percies and the Scots in their incessant revolts against Henry IV. Bishop Strickland's name is honourably connected in his diocese with various good works: the traveller to the North on leaving Penrith by the London and Northwestern Railway still sees to his left, parallel to the line, the water-course by which Strickland supplied the people of that town with water. In Penrith he must have been much interested, as he founded a chantry there. He also did much work at his cathedral, and at his palace of Rose. From whence he obtained the money, it is hard to say, for Cumberland was so wasted and impoverished by the Scots that the king had, in 1402, to remit all taxes and debts due to the crown. Bishop Strickland died in 1419, and was buried in his cathedral in accordance with the provisions of his will, which is printed in the *Testamenta Eboracensia* by the Surtees Society. He was succeeded by another local man, Roger Whelpdale, a native of Greystoke, of high distinction and office at his university of Oxford, and the writer of books on logic and mathematics. He was appointed by papal provision, and then elected by the chapter of Carlisle under the king's licence. He died in 1422 at Carlisle Place in London. His lengthy will is also printed among the *Testamenta Eboracensia*, and by it he bequeaths books, vestments, and money to Queen's and Balliol Colleges, Oxford, and £20 to the scholars of that university; he also left £200 for the endowment of a chantry in his cathedral in memory of Sir Thomas Skelton, and Mr. John Glaston, both natives of the diocese. William Barrow, bishop of Bangor, another distinguished Oxford man, was translated by papal provision to the vacant see: he died in 1429, and was buried in his cathedral: his monument is in the south aisle. Marmaduke Lumley was elected to the see by the chapter, confirmed by the king, and approved of by the pope. He suffered much from the devastation of his see by the Scots, and was translated to Lincoln in 1449. To him succeeded, by papal provision, Nicholas Close, archdeacon of Colchester, who had done good service in procuring a treaty with Scotland. He was translated to Lichfield in 1451, and died in that year. During his episcopate the prior and convent of Carlisle *zelo piæ devotionis accensi* conceived the project of placing in their cathedral—*ymaginem sive statuam ejusdem Virginis laminis argenteis superornandis auro, gemmis, monilibus multisque aliis ornamentis pretiosis.* The project was not carried out; an indulgence to donors to the image is recorded in the registers at York, but is marked—*non emanavit.*—Surtees Society, vol. xliv.

Next came, by papal provision, William Percy, who died in 1462: John Kingscott, elected by the chapter and approved by the pope, who died in 1463: Richard Scrope, by papal provision, who died in 1468; his brief nuncupative will is printed in the *Testamenta Eboracensia.* Edward Story, probably a local man, succeeded, who was translated to Chichester in 1477, where his register, full of interesting information concerning the state of his new diocese, makes us much to regret that his Carlisle register does not exist. He was a man of great liberality. Richard Bell, prior of Durham, came next, by papal provision, known to fame for his tower at Rose, and his magnificent brass in his cathedral. He died in 1496, and William Severn, a Benedictine, abbot of St. Mary's, York, followed, and was translated to Durham in 1502. Roger Leyburn, of the Leyburns of Cunswick, in Westmorland, then held the see to 1508, when came John Penny, bishop of

Bangor, who died in 1520. It would be superfluous to give a catalogue of the treaties with Scotland, at the foot of which will be found the name of one or another of the bishops thus rapidly enumerated. The century and a quarter over which their successive tenures of office extend cover much of fascinating interest in English history,—the battle of Agincourt, the conquest of France, its subsequent loss and the end of the Hundred Years' War, the Wars of the Roses, the advent of the New Monarchy, the introduction of the printing-press and of the new learning, the battle of Flodden, &c.; but there is nothing special to be said of the diocese of Carlisle. The North of England, under Clifford influence, was largely Lancastrian in feeling, but Carlisle was held by the Yorkists in 1461, when the Lancastrians besieged it, burnt its suburbs, and so impoverished the place, that Edward IV. remitted, by charter, to the citizens for the future one-half of their fee-farm rent of £80. The people in the diocese must have been poor, ignorant, and barbarous. Æneas Sylvius Piccolomini, in an account of his adventures (which has generally been considered to belong to the East Marches, and not to the West, but which internal evidence proves to relate to the West),[1] describes the people at a place on the Solway at which he landed, either Bowness-on-Solway or Burgh-on-Sands, as never having seen wine or white bread, crowding to look at him as a novelty, and asking if he was a Christian. Chastity they cared

[1] See Cadwallader J. Bates, on "The Border Holds of Northumberland," in "Archæologia Eliana," vol. xiv. pp. 1, 7.

nothing for, and the country he describes as "rugged, uncultivated, and in winter sunless." At this place he stayed all night in a cottage and supped with his host and the priest, of whom he tells us nothing, except that he and all the men took refuge nightly in a tower against the incursions of the Scots, leaving the women outside.

CHAPTER VIII.

THE REFORMATION.

In 1521 John Kyte, archbishop of Armagh, relinquished that piece of preferment for the titular archbishopric of Thebes, in Greece, together with the bishopric of Carlisle. Kyte, a Londoner by birth, had held the office of sub-dean of the Royal Chapel, and had been sent ambassador to Spain by Henry VII. He was made Archbishop of Armagh by papal provision in 1513, and his translation to Thebes and Carlisle was effected by the influence of Cardinal Wolsey, whose friendship Kyte requited by continuing steadfast to him even in his adversity. It is worth while to mention that the fees demanded by the Papal Court on Kyte's translation amounted to 1890 ducats. In the tariff issued in 1511, on authority of Charles the Bold, Duke of Burgundy, the papal ducat is valued at 33 groats, so we get £1,039. 10s. as the demand made upon Kyte, or two years' income of the see of Carlisle, which in the *Valor* of Henry VIII. is estimated at £541. No wonder the nation had long groaned under such exactions, and under the large sums which were drawn from their pockets for probates and mortuaries by bishops and priests, too often imposed upon them by foreign authority. We have seen what a large proportion of the bishops of Carlisle were appointed by papal provision; their fourteenth-century registers contain one (if not more) brief from the Papal Court, ordering the prior and convent of Carlisle to find a benefice for a priest who is named, and the wills in these registers speak to the severity of the mortuaries.

Bishop Kyte was, as matter of course, in various commissions to treat with the Scots. He acted with Wolsey in the matter of the king's divorce, and he sided with Lee, archbishop of York, in opposing Archbishop Cranmer and the reforming party. He built largely at Rose Castle, but died in London in 1537. He was succeeded by Robert Oldridge,[1] or Aldridge, a scholar, poet, and orator, provost of Eton, and holder of many offices, which are detailed in the county histories. He was one of the authors of the "Bishop's Book," but in his opinions he disagreed with Cranmer and the reformers, and sided with Lee, Gardiner, and Tunstall. He died in 1555, at Horncastle; and he had a gift from Henry VIII. of a house at Lambeth Marsh, called Carlisle House, for use of himself and his successors.

The episcopates of these two bishops, covering the greater part of the reign of Henry VIII. and the reign of Edward VI., are not so devoid of local colour as were those of their predecessors.

The causes which for long had been preparing men's minds for the inevitableness of some sort of reformation of the Church of England, would be slowly felt in a poor and remote diocese like Carlisle, whose clergy were probably the most ignorant in England, but still there must have been a few among

[1] He is called Oldridge in the charter of foundation of the Dean and Chapter of Carlisle.

them who had tasted of the "New Learning," and read the works of Erasmus and Colet. There is no evidence that the inhabitants of Cumberland and Westmorland were particularly anxious for any sweeping changes; on the contrary, we shall see that they were not, if we may judge from what they afterwards did on occasion of the suppression of the smaller religious houses, or those having incomes under £200 per annum. The Act of 1536 for the suppression of these was preceded by some sort of visitation made by commissioners; the results are generally supposed to have been laid before Parliament, in a book called the Black Book, afterwards destroyed (so the story goes) by Bishop Bonnor at command of Queen Mary. Some fragments which escaped bear the title of "Comperta," and very shocking they are.

The story of the Black Book, and of the Comperta, has been very carefully sifted by Canon Dixon in the first volume of his History of the Church of England, and he arrives at conclusions very unfavourable to those documents. They have been recently thoroughly exposed by Father Gasquet in "Henry VIII. and the English Monasteries."[1] But, be these documents true or false, laid before Parliament or not, the act for the suppression of the smaller houses was passed. Locally it affected all the religious houses in the diocese of Carlisle but St. Mary's, Carlisle, and Holm Cultram. The discontent occasioned by the suppression of these houses,

---

[1] London: John Hodges, 1888.

co-operating with other grievances, and assiduously fanned by the monks and priests, set the North of England on fire. In October, 1536, a rebellion of some sixty thousand persons rose in Lincolnshire, and subsided in a fortnight. It was followed by the rising in Yorkshire, known as "Aske's Rebellion," or "The Pilgrimage of Grace," and on October 13, the beacons of Cumberland and Westmorland blazed out in response to the fires on the Yorkshire hills. The Pilgrimage found sympathisers and promoters in the diocese of Carlisle. Robert Jerby, abbot of Holm Cultram, Towneley, chancellor of Carlisle, the prior of Lanercost, and a nameless vicar of Penrith, made themselves especially obnoxious to the king by their activity. Carlisle was held for the king by Sir Thomas Clifford and Sir Christopher Dacre; certain unfounded suspicions about Dacre's fidelity were evidently in circulation, but he in the end thoroughly vindicated it. Penrith appears to have been the local *focus* of insurrection, and thither repaired Abbot Jerby, and there he aided and abetted in the sending men to the insurgents at York. He warned his tenants of the manor of Holm Cultram, on pain of hanging, to attend illegal gatherings at Wayttyrighow (?) and on Broadfield, and, when on February 12, 1536-7, some eight thousand rabble from Kendal, Richmond, Kirkby Stephen, Appleby, and Hexham, under Nichol Musgrave, laid siege to Carlisle, he rode with them and acted as their commissioner to demand the surrender of the town. Clifford and Dacre repulsed and pursued the disorderly assailants, who rallied and made a stand, but melted away in panic on hearing of the approach of the royal forces under the Duke of Norfolk. That leader proclaimed martial law in Cumberland, Westmorland, Durham, and the northern angle of Yorkshire by displaying the royal banner. A courier was despatched to Henry VIII. with the news, and he replied in a letter which has been often quoted, and which is printed at full length by the Surtees Society, volume xliv. p. 150; this volume also contains other documents, of which we have been making free use. One passage we reproduce :—

"Our pleasure is, that before you shall close upp our said baner again, you shal, in any wise, cause suche dredfull execution to be doon upon a good nombre of th' inhabitauntes of every toune, village, and hamlet, that have offended in this rebellion, as well by the hanging them up in trees, as by the quartering of them and the setting of their heddes and quarters in every toune, greate and small, and in all suche other places, as they may be a ferefull spectacle to all other hereafter, that wold practise any like mater."

The letter also orders the duke to get and send the vicar of Penrith and chancellor Towneley to the king, and to visit

"Salleye (Sawley), Hexam, Newminster, Leonerdecaste, Saincte Agathe, and all such other places as have made any maner of resistence or in any wise conspired or kept their houses with any force sithens th' appointement at Doncastre, you shall, without pitie or circumstance, nowe that our baner is displayed, cause all the monkes and chanons, that be in anywise faultie, to be tyed uppe, without further delay or ceremoney, to the terrible example of others."

The abbot of Sawley and the prior of Hexham were certainly hanged; the fate of the other three is not known, nor what became of Chancellor Towneley and the vicar of Penrith. Seventy-four persons were executed in the towns of Cumberland and Westmorland; by some oversight they were not hanged in chains, as were the insurgents who endured that fate in Yorkshire and the bishopric of Durham: "the bodies were cut down and buried by certain women," to the anger of the duke. Nothing is said as to the fate of the abbot of Holm Cultram, but as Sir Thomas Wharton writes, in August, 1537, of "the dethe of the laytt Abbot of Holm," he was probably hanged, unless he cheated the wood by dying. Sir Thomas Wharton, in his letter, also says he had attended the assizes in Cumberland:—

"when dyvers henyus ryottes ande oyer unlawfull demenors er laytly doune. Ther is on grett ryott foundon to be doune by the commandment of the byschoppe off Kerlesle."

This was compromising for Bishop Kyte, as pointing to his complicity with the insurgents, but Kyte was beyond the king's power; he died in London, June 19, 1537.

The Pilgrimage of Grace was but a vain performance: it originated in discontent with the suppression of the small houses; it failed to save them, and it furnished the excuse for the suppression of the larger houses, whose various abbots and inmates had encouraged it. The punishment of Holm Cultram was not long delayed: it has been conjectured that Abbot Jerby was hanged; his successor, Abbot Gawen Borrowdale, surrendered the abbey to the king on the 5th or 6th of March, 1538, the commissioner to receive the surrender being Dr. Legh. Borrowdale was appointed the first rector, his brethren were pensioned off, and the fabric of the church was permitted to stand as "a grete ayde socor and defence" for the parishioners against the Scots, to become the melancholy victim of storm, fire, neglect, and churchwardens that it now is.

The priory of Wetheral was surrendered to the king on October 20, 1539, and the priory of St. Mary's, Carlisle, on January 9, 1540. Dr. Layton was the commissioner who received the surrender of Carlisle. Out of the dissolved priory of Carlisle, and on the site thereof, by charter bearing date May 8, 1541, the king founded the Cathedral Church of the Holy and Undivided Trinity of Carlisle, and created a dean and four prebendaries one body corporate under the name of the Dean and Chapter of the said cathedral church. Launcelot Salkeld, the last prior, a man defamed in the worthless "Comperta," was appointed the first dean. By another charter, bearing date May 6 of the same year, the king endowed the Dean and Chapter with most of the revenues of the dissolved priory of Carlisle, as well as with all the revenues of the dissolved priory, or cell of Wetheral, which had heretofore been attached to St. Mary's Abbey at York. On June 6, 1545, the king, under the Act (31 Hen. VIII. c. 9) authorising the foundation of additional bishoprics, delivered to the Dean and Chapter of Carlisle a body of statutes by the hands of his commissioners, and signed by them, but not under the Great Seal.

These statutes have given rise to some important

and well-known lawsuits, and were the primary cause of the passing of the Act 6 Anne, c. 21, by which the validity of the statutes of the cathedrals of the New Foundation was established. The original copy of these statutes delivered by the commissioners of Henry VIII. is not in existence, but an examined and certified copy of the time of Charles II. is kept in a chest in the Treasury; this copy has been printed in 1879 by the Dean and Chapter, under the supervision of the Ven. Archdeacon Prescott and the late Canon Chalker, and a translation, with a most valuable preface and notes, was published by the archdeacon in the same year. Of these we hope later on to avail ourselves.

Oldridge, or Aldridge, or Adrich, Kyte's successor in the bishopric of Carlisle, was one of the bishops who supported in Parliament the "Act for Abolishing of Diversity of Opinions," known as the "Statute of the Six Articles," and "The Whip with Six Strings." The persecutions under the statute were mainly in the south of England; possibly the seventy-four examples that the Duke of Norfolk had tied up in the two counties of Cumberland and Westmorland were not forgotten, and further severity was unnecessary.

In 1542 war broke out between England and Scotland. James V. being on the side of Rome, was unfavourable to his uncle, the English king, whose policy was to renew the claims made by Edward I. to superiority over the kingdom of Scotland. A Scottish army entered the West Marches of England and was put to rout on the 24th November, 1542, by a few hundred borderers under Sir Thomas Dacre the

Bastard, and Jack Musgrave, of Bewcastle, both of whom Mr. Froude elevates into lords. Sir Thomas Dacre was rewarded in the following year by a grant of some of the possessions of the dissolved House of Lanercost.

Henry VIII. died January 28, 1547, leaving a boy of nine years old to succeed him. By his will he clearly intended, in the selection of his executors, to leave a government behind him in which, as Mr. Froude says, the parties of reaction and progress should alike be represented, and should form a check one upon another. But the Earl of Hertford managed to modify the scheme, and, with the title of Duke of Somerset, to be made Protector of the kingdom. He strengthened his influence over the nation by a victory over the Scots at Pinkie, near Musselburgh, and he gave his support to the advanced Reformers. The Six Articles, and the Acts against the Lollards were repealed; a general visitation of the kingdom was held, which was divided into six circuits, each with its own commissioners. But the changes this visitation was intended to enforce; the history of the first and second prayer-books of Edward VI.; the fall of Somerset and the rise of Northumberland; the death of the young king, and the tragic fate of the unfortunate Lady Jane Grey,—all belong to general history and not to that of the diocese of Carlisle. One important document of this reign has been published by the Cumberland and Westmorland Society (Transactions, vol. viii.), namely, the inventory of church goods in Cumberland, taken under a Royal Commission issued in 1552. The commissioners were Sir Thomas Dacre and Sir Richard Musgrave, Kts., and William Pykerynge, Thomas Salkeld, Robert Lamplugh, and Anthony Burnis, Esquires. The contents of this document strikingly indicate the poverty of the county, if this inventory is compared with those for Berkshire and Herefordshire, which are published by James Parker, London; still, nearly every church had "one chalice of silver," but, chalices apart, the silver vessels in the 111 churches visited were only two paten covers, one broken cross, and one pyx. Eight churches had tin chalices, two had none, and only one church had cruets, and those of tin. The commissioners carried away or disposed of for the king's use all church goods beyond a very limited supply.

The innovations introduced in the reign of Edward VI. were intensely unpopular, and people were eager to recur to the old practices as soon as the opportunity presented itself. At Naworth Castle is a book entitled:—

"*Hynorum (sic) cum notis opusculum ad usum Sar.' diurno servitio per totū annū apprime necessariū ; plurimis eliminatis mēdis.* Antwerp, 1528, *per Christopherū Endoviensen.*"

On the title page is written :—

"*Dūs Henricus Browne me possidet.*"

Below :—

"*Tho. Riding est possesor.*"

On back of titlepage is :—

"*Tertio die Septembris anno dñi* 1553, *fuit missa iterum incipienda in Ecclia Sci Cuthberti in fyt* (?) *in civitate Carl.*"

Just six weeks after Mary was proclaimed queen,

which was on the 19th of July, 1553. A further inscription tells us more about Henry Browne :—

"*Dñs Henricus Browne capellanus curatusque Ecclie Sant Cuthbert Carl. et decanus decanatus Carl., &c.*"—SURTEES SOCIETY, vol. lxviii., p. 477.

This book is some evidence that the use in the diocese of Carlisle was the Use of Sarum. The missal still survives which was presented, in 1506, by Robert Cooke, apparently a priest, to the church of Caldbeck, in Cumberland, together with a silver chalice and pax, and some vestments, as detailed in a Latin note written in the book. It is of the Use of Sarum, and the Mass of St. Mungo (to whom Caldbeck Church is dedicated), is in manuscript at the end. This fine volume, in 1880, was in possession of the Benedictine mission at Warwick Bridge, near Carlisle. We believe it is now at Ushaw. Dr. Prescott, in his translation of the Statutes of Carlisle Cathedral, shows that the offices enjoined by the statutes of Henry VIII. were to be in accordance with the Use of Sarum.

However eagerly people might welcome the restoration of Mass, and of laws against heresy, they obstinately refused to restore the Church lands, and they clung obstinately to the royal supremacy. The unhappy queen could not prevail upon them : her persecutions created sympathy for those she and Bonnor sent to the stake. She dragged the country into an unwilling war to support her unpopular husband, and had she not died when she did, in 1558, there would have been a general revolt. Bishop

Oldridge, or Aldridge, preceded her, dying in 1556, and Dr. Owen Oglethorpe succeeded him. Oglethorpe was president of Magdalen College, Oxford, and first canon and then dean of Windsor; and he and his predecessor were both among the theologians to whom Cranmer had addressed the questions, on the answers to which the Third English Confession was founded, viz., "The Necessary Doctrine and Erudition of a Christian Man." Oglethorpe had been on the previous commission of 1540, but he is best known as having officiated at the coronation of Queen Elizabeth,—Pole, the Archbishop of Canterbury, having died on the same day as Queen Mary, while the Archbishop of York (Heath), alarmed by the proposal to use the English Litany, refused to officiate. With the other Marian bishops, except Kitchen of Llandaff, Oglethorpe was deprived of his see, for refusing the oath of supremacy, in May, 1559.

By the influence of the Earl of Bedford and of Bishop Sandys (Bishop of Worcester, afterwards Archbishop of York), the see of Carlisle was offered to a distinguished member of a distinguished Westmorland family, Barnard Gilpin, rector of Houghton-le-Spring, and a kinsman of Sandys. Sandys was himself a member of a Cumberland family, though born at Hawkshead, in Lancashire, and he was educated at St. Bees School, in Cumberland, in company with Grindal, a native of the parish of St. Bees, and in succession Bishop of London, Archbishop of York, and Archbishop of Canterbury in the reign of Queen Elizabeth. A well-informed antiquary writes :—"The fact that both Grindal and Sandys became brilliant ornaments of the Reformed Church, would seem to suggest that their teacher at St. Bees must have been a man of Protestant tendencies."[1] Both these prelates were born in the limits of the extended diocese of Carlisle; obscure, wild, and popish as that district must have been in the sixteenth century, yet two of its sons greatly influenced the character of the reformed Church of England. Sandys must have known well the sort of man that the diocese of Carlisle wanted, and in his letter to Gilpin, announcing that the queen had nominated the latter bishop of Carlisle, he strongly urges acceptance of the offer :—

"I am not ignorant that your inclination rather delighteth in the peaceable tranquility of a private life. But if you looke upon the estate of the Church of England with a respective eye, you cannot, with a good conscience, refuse this charge imposed upon you; so much the lesse, because it is in such a place, as wherein no man is found fitter then yourselfe to deserve well of the Church."

Gilpin resolutely declined, and the reason he gave was, that

"he refused not so much the bishopricke as the inconvenience of the place, for if I had bene chosen in this kinde to any bishopricke elsewhere, I would not have refused it; but in that place I have been willing to avoide the trouble of it, seeing I had there manie of my freinds and kindred, at whom I must connive in many thinges, not without hurte to myselfe, or else deny them manie thinges, not without offence to them."[2]

---

[1] "Archbishop Grindal, and his Grammar School of Saint Bees," by William Jackson, F.S.A.

[2] For much of the above the author is indebted to Collingwood's "Memoirs of Bernard Gilpin."

It is probable that Gilpin thought he could not advance the reformed religion in the diocese of Carlisle, in opposition to his extensive family connexions there. Less charitable persons have suggested that as Houghton-le-Spring was worth about £400 a year, and the bishopric of Carlisle only, according to Strype, £268 (a falling off from the value in the *Valor* of Henry VIII. of £541), other reasons might have moved Gilpin.

The bishops that Queen Elizabeth, during her long reign, appointed to Carlisle, were John Best, 1560; Richard Barnes, 1570; John Meye, 1577; and Henry Robinson, 1598. The deans of Carlisle appointed by Queen Elizabeth were Sir Thomas Smith, whom she appointed at her accession, or rather re-appointed, for he had held the deanery during the reign of Edward VI., after the ejection of Lancelot Salkeld, who was re-appointed by Queen Mary on the ejection of Smith. Sir Thomas Smith was a deacon only; to him succeeded in 1577 Sir John Wooley, and in 1596 Sir Christopher Perkins, who held it until 1622; these two were both laymen. There is no evidence that these deans, very distinguished men they were, and holders of high office at the universities, in state and in diplomacy, ever saw the deanery they enjoyed. The deanery of Carlisle was, in fact, secularised throughout the reign of Queen Elizabeth, and for part of that of James I. Accounts of these deans are in *Archæologia*, vol. xxxviii., where it appears Smith got £80 from his deanery, after paying Salkeld £40 as pension. This secularisation of the deanery was probably one of the things Bernard Gilpin disliked the idea of conniving at.

To return to the Elizabethan bishops, John Best, Yorkshire by birth, Oxford by education, and the first Protestant bishop of Carlisle, found his see no bed of roses. In a letter to Cecil, Bishop Best writes that thirteen or fourteen of his rectors and vicars refused to appear at his general visitation in 1561, and take the oath of allegiance, while in many churches in his diocese Mass continued to be said under the countenance and open protection of Lord Dacre; the clergy of the diocese he described as wicked imps of Antichrist, ignorant, stubborn, and past measure, false and subtile. Fear only, he said, would make them obedient, and Lord Cumberland and Lord Dacre would not allow him to meddle with them. In 1562 the same bishop complained that, between Lord Dacre and the Earls of Cumberland and Westmorland, " God's glorious gospel could not take place in the counties under their rule." The few Protestants " durst not be known for fear of a shrewd turn;" and the lords and magistrates looked through their fingers while the law was openly defied. The county was full of wishings and wagers for the alteration of religion; rumours and tales of the Spaniards and Frenchmen to come in for the reformation of the same; while the articles of the secret league between the Guises and Spain for the extirpation of heresy circulated in manuscript in the houses of the northern gentlemen.[1] The Bishop of London, Grindal, in a letter dated Dec. 27, 1563, in which he

[1] The bishop's letters are cited by Mr. Froude. The author has not, owing to ill health, been able to see the volume of " Domestic Calendars " in which they occur.

begs Cecil to appoint a Mr. Scot to a vacant prebend at Carlisle, says:—

"The Bishop of Carlisle hath complained to me for want of preachers in his diocese. All his prebendaries are ignorant priests, or old, unlearned monks."

In another letter he says:—

"I pray you be good to my lord of Carlisle (*i.e.*, Bishop Best) the bringer. There be marvellous practices to deface him in my lawless country."

As mentioned before, Grindal was a native of the parish of St. Bees. Best's troubles must have been increased in 1568, when Mary, queen of Scots, landed in Cumberland and was conducted to Carlisle Castle, a virtual prisoner, by Mr. (afterwards Sir) Richard Lowther, deputy to the Lord Warden, Lord Scrope. To Carlisle also repaired the Earl of Northumberland, who demanded that the queen should be handed over to his custody, and who, when Lowther declined to do so, abused that gentleman in very rough terms. Carlisle became the centre of intrigue among the papal party, but the gentry of Cumberland and Westmorland showed no enthusiasm whatever in the queen's behalf, though their two counties and Northumberland were then reckoned the stronghold of English Catholicism. After a stay of two months, Queen Mary was removed, in July, 1568, to Bolton, in Yorkshire. In the following year the "Rising of the North" took place under the Earls of Northumberland and Westmorland, who again reared the banner that had been flown in "the Pilgrimage of Grace." Their objects were to rescue the Queen of Scots, to subvert the government of Elizabeth, and to re-establish the ancient faith. One of the instigators of this outbreak was Leonard Dacre, uncle of the little lad on whose untimely death, caused by the fall of a vaulting horse, the great estate of Dacre of the North had fallen to three co-heiresses. Leonard Dacre "stomached it much," says Camden, "that so goodly an inheritance should fall to his nieces." He assumed the title of Lord Dacre, and claimed the estates as heir in tail male. He instigated the two earls to rise; then betrayed them to Elizabeth, whom he persuaded to entrust to him a share in putting down the rising. He seized his nieces' estates, fortified Naworth Castle, and collected some 3,000 men who rallied to the old border slogan of "A read Bull, a read Bull." Lord Scrope, relying on Dacre's loyalty, moved out from Carlisle to intercept the two earls, should they march for Scotland, leaving Bishop Best in command of the castle of Carlisle. He was recalled by rumour of a plot to seize the castle and murder the bishop. The rising soon became a flight: the two earls arrived as fugitives at Naworth, where the wily Dacre gave them but short shelter; he was in no mood to compromise himself, and the earls fled to Liddisdale. But the queen had discovered Dacre's double dealings: she gave Lord Hunsdon peremptory orders to apprehend that "cankred subtill traitor," as she called him. Hunsdon and Dacre met one another at Gelt Bridge, about four miles from Naworth: Dacre was worsted and fled into exile. The gentry of Cumberland and

Westmorland had stood aloof from the rising: perhaps they remembered too well the seventy-four hung by the Duke of Norfolk, perhaps they mistrusted Leonard Dacre. On Lord Hunsdon's intercession the queen pardoned the borderers who fought for Dacre. The Earl of Northumberland was brought to the scaffold, and more than 600 of his followers were executed. Locally "The Rising of the North" is known as "Dacre's Raid."

Bishop Best died in 1570. Barnes, who succeeded him, had been one of Archbishop Grindal's chaplains, and was canon and chancellor of York, and after holding the see of Carlisle for seven years was translated to Durham. In 1571 Grindal issued his injunction for the substitution of "cups" for chalices; the number of cups of that date in the diocese of Carlisle shows that Barnes enforced this injunction in his own see. At Crosthwaite, in Cumberland, the church was still, in 1571, in possession of a large number of vestments and a quantity of plate, which had escaped the commissioners of Edward VI., or had been restored by the commissioners of Queen Mary. Bishop Barnes issued a most peremptory injunction to the churchwardens and others, ordering all the plate to be sold before December 1, the vestments to be sold or cut up to cover cushions, and that with the proceeds fine linen cloths, for the communion table, and a covering of buckram, fringed, were to be got before Christmas, and also two fair large communion cups with covers, one fine diaper napkin for the communion and sacramental bread, and two fair pots or flagons of tin for the wine.

We thus have Bishop Barnes's directions as to the altar furniture necessary for one of his largest churches. Similar injunctions by him probably lurk in other parish chests.[1] He also held the first recorded visitation of the cathedral under the statutes of Henry VIII.; in it he ordered certain minor canons, suspected of papism, to recite on certain days in St. Mary's Church, Carlisle, in an audible voice, during divine service, after the Apostles' Creed, the English Confession, entitled " A Declaration of Certain Principal Articles of Religion." He also enjoins a newly-appointed *Theologic Prelector* of the cathedral to preach *ad Clerum* every year, as well as at other times.

Bishop Barnes was succeeded by John Meye, master of Catherine Hall, Cambridge, who held the see for twenty years. He died in 1597, during a visitation of the plague. Some records exist of the proceedings in Cumberland of the Court of High Commission in the northern parts during the episcopate of Bishop Meye, who was one of the commissioners in Cumberland, as were Lord Scroop of Bolton, Warden of the West Marches, and certain local clerks, knights, and esquires. They held their sittings at Carlisle and Rose Castles, and in St. Mary's Church at Carlisle. It appears that the commissioners issued articles of inquiry addressed

---

[1] On the Edwardian and Marian Commissioners, and on Barnes's injunction to Crosthwaite, see "Old Church Plate in the Diocese of Carlisle," published by Cumberland and Westmorland Archæological Society.

probably to the clergyman or the churchwardens, who in reply made presentments of offenders. The following are specimens :—

"John Adamson presented to be a drunkard. He hath not receyvid (the Sacrament) sence Easter—he cometh not to churche.

William Smyth, Curate of Edenhall, presented to wear his hose lowse at the knees.

William Mester presented to be a drunkard and rayler against ministers and wifes.

Robert Gibson, Agnes Strichet, and Agnes Morehous, presented that they have not receyved thrise this yeare because they could not saye the Ten Commandments. [These parties were ordered to learn the Commandments, the Lord's Prayer, and the Creed before next Easter.]

John Dockher for playing on his pipes when the Curat was at evening prayer.

Anna Harrison, widow, suspected of witchecrafte.

Anthony Huggen presented for medicioning children with miniting a hammer as a smith of kynde.[1]

Janet Huggen presinted to be a sorcerer and medicioner of children.

Maria Hutton alias Skelton, a widow lady, presented for wearing beads.

Margaret, wife of Richard Jackson, presented for fasting St. Anthonie's fast.

John Taylor presented for suspect of sorcerie for that he had knyt in cows taile staves, salt, and herbes.

Henry Willson, Curat of Holm Cultram, presented for drunkennes and playing at cardes and tables at sundrie times.

---

[1] The child was placed on an anvil, and the smith with the heavy sledge-hammer made as if he would crush the child with a blow. The hammer was allowed to descend upon it, but stayed in time, so as not to touch it.

Robert Winter presented that he is a malicious person and beareth evell will against his neighbour.

Thomas Hodgson presented for ringing a bell at the last floode to provoke people to prayer.

John Stricket for that he gave George Mashall S^d in the weeke for the lone of 20/ [Usury].

Agnes Watson for keping a dead man's scalpe.

Robert Sanderson for medicioning for the worme.

Hugh Askewe for burying a quick nowt, and a dogg, and a quick cock [a charm].

Alice Thompson presented that she will not learn the catechism.

Jenkin Swan presented for casting his glove downe in the churche [Irthington] and offering to fight with any one that would put furth the hand.

Janet Walker of Lanercost presented that she hath had 4 bastards. Christopher Dacre and Thomas Carleton, officers of Gillesland, ordered to bring her up. She appears, and is ordered to do penance in Carlisle market-place the next Saturday and in the parish churche.

Agnes wife of John Wyse, alias Winkan John Wyse, presented to be a medicioner for the waffe of an ill winde and for the fayryes.

Mabell, wyffe of John Browne, presented to be a witche and taketh mylke from kye.

Margaret, wife of Nicholas Gyll, presented that she liveth in disquietnes with her husband in banning and scolding.

William Forster for fornication with Janet Mowse, and because he can't say the catechism.

The Churchwardens of Irthington, for that the churchyard layd common unfensed, the church porch downe, the surplesse rent, the Bible rent, no Commandments set upp, and they would presente none for not coming to Churche.

The Curat of Lanercost for that he married two cupples of folkes in a prophane place without bannes asking.

Margaret Avery, of Lanercost, presented for cursing her father and mother.

The Churchwardens of Denton presented that they come

not to churche neither levie the penalties nor presente the absente."[1]

A thoroughly competent authority on the condition of the diocese of Carlisle thus comments on the presentments just quoted :—

"When such were the fruits the ill-condition of the country may be imagined. How, indeed, could it be otherwise? The ancient religious establishments had been swept away, and little or nothing done to supply their place. To earnest religious reformers the suppression of monasteries and the triumph of Protestantism might afford satisfaction to cover every other shortcoming. But these were the minority. To the bulk of the people the transaction seemed more like plunder. They beheld the ancient possessors turned out, their habitations and churches dilapidated,—one rapacious grantee of the Crown stripping off the lead, another overhauling the furniture and decorations, a third, perhaps, carrying away the very stones to rear for himself a mansion on the fair domain he had the luck or the interest to obtain out of the sequestered estates of the Church. Little or no care was taken to make provision for the spiritual wants of those numerous parishes which the religious houses had held appropriate and had served by their brethren. What could be the effect of this on the popular mind but to induce a feeling of indifference and a disbelief in the reality and efficacy of any religious establishment whatever, and hence a falling away to ignorance and superstition of the grossest kind.

"Perhaps a more perfect instance of this reckless method of dealing with the property of the Church cannot be found than in the parishes of Lanercost, Farlam, and Over

---

[1] These are quoted from "Gillesland," a tract published by Lonsdale at Carlisle without author's name or date, but written by the G. G. Mounsey, late registrar of the diocese of Carlisle, and secretary to several bishops of that see.

Denton. Every acre of land, every dwelling and erection within them belonging to the Church, all tithes and pecuniary dues were seized by the Crown. Some portion of land near the Abbey yet remains so, having been granted to Sir Thomas Dacre and his heirs male, and having fallen in again to the Crown on failure of such. The remainder was granted in fee without any stipulation or expressed condition for the grantees to provide for the parochial cures. It was not to be expected that they would voluntarily do so, but surely it ought to have been specifically enjoined. Generally speaking, these grantees were either Court favourites or greedy speculators who purchased of the Crown. Neither the one nor the other cared for aught but to make the most for themselves. They pocketed the whole proceeds, and refused to pay the miserable ecclesiastic more than the meagre fee or allowance which the monastery had formerly given to the brother who took the duty. The law made no provision for compelling them to allow a decent maintenance to a sufficient minister."

The reader will learn more about the parishes of Lanercost, Farlam, and Over Denton when he comes to the chapter on the eighteenth century.

Bishop Meye was succeeded by Henry Robinson, a native of Carlisle, educated at Queen's College, Oxford, of which he became provost. In 1598 one Christopher Robinson was executed for high treason at Carlisle, on account of exercising his functions in England as a Roman Catholic priest. He was born at Woodside, near Wigton, and educated abroad: Bishop Robinson visited him while in confinement prior to his execution. This is the only instance in the diocese of Carlisle of martyrdom for religious opinions unconnected with actual rebellion. Bishop Robinson is commemorated in his cathedral and in his college by a small brass (in duplicate) which has frequently been engraved. He died in 1616, and, like his predecessor, of the plague. The next five bishops of Carlisle were Robert Snowden, 1616–1621; Richard Milburn, translated from St. David's, 1621–1624; Richard Senhouse, 1624–1626; Francis White, dean of Carlisle, appointed bishop in 1626 and translated to Norwich in 1628; Barnaby Potter, provost of Queen's, Oxford, 1628 to 1641. There is little special to relate of the see of Carlisle during their episcopates. Milburn, Senhouse, and Potter were local men. Snowden was, we fancy, but with hesitation, the first married bishop of Carlisle. Mrs. Snowden appears in the accounts of the chamberlains of Carlisle as partaking of the hospitality of the mayor and aldermen. The following interesting letter from Bishop Snowden to James I. was found by Mr. Walter Money, F.S.A., among papers collected by Mr. John Packer, secretary to George Villiers, first Duke of Buckingham:—

"Most blessed Soveraigne, my great and most gratious Lord and Ma.,

"All yor Subjects stand infinitely obliged in their services to yr highnes, but my self farr beyond many Thousands. I have therefore coveted to be the first in my congratulations and thanksgivings to the God of heaven for yr Ma'ties good health and safe returne unto us.

"When I made professions of my homage in the Pallace of Newmarket, your Ma'tie most graciously required me to write unto yor selfe immediately.

"To the end I myght inable myselfe for that kind of most happie service I have since my first coming to Rose Castle (the only place of habitacon left unto me by my predecessors), for the space of well nere two moneths by my presence in visitations, sessions, and commissions, and by petitions, conference, and suggestions, gained some notice of the Civil and Ecclesiastique state of my Diocesse, and I have found that

"1. The Citie of Carlisle is in great ruine, and extreme poverty, partly because the Lieutenant is not there resiant, and partly for that ye Inhabitants exercise themselves in no Arts or trades, neither have they other meanes of livelyhood besides fishing.

"2. In the country at large many of the meaner sort, live dispersedly in Cottages, or little farmes, scarcely sufficient for their necessary maintenance, whereby idleness, thefts, and robberies are occasioned. And according to the nature of the soile, and qualitie of the air (like that in Norfolke) the vulgar people are subtill, violent, litigious, and pursuers of endless suites by appeales, to their utter impoverishment, and the poor wretches finde admittance of their most unreasonable appeales, both at York and London, for which those higher courts deserve to be blamed.

"3. The gentry have beene formerly induced to straighten themselves by intrigues and bribes, whereby they have inclined to partialities in publique negotiations, howbeit I find the most of them flexible to good motions, saving that they are divided in their dependancies upon eminent persons, but their factiones may perhaps be for some purposes convenient, as they are for others inconvenient. Yr Ma'ties oracle-like wisdome will easily conceive the meaning of this parable by their various and repugnant answers to yor propositions touching the government of the lowest parts, of one of those answeres I could get no copie, but copies of the rest I have sent in a packett to the Earl of Buckingham, to the end Yr Ma'tie may at your pleasure command the sight of them before that they shall be exhibited or presented with subscription.

"4. The state ecclesiastique is hugely weakened not onely by Impropriations served by poor Vicars, and multitudes of base hirelings, but by compositions contracted in the troubled times, and now prescribed, yet there are some show of grave and learned pastors. And albeit many of them in their habits and external inconformities seme to be Puritanes, yet have I not found any of repugnant opinion to any of our summons or lawes ecclesiastical.

"And though my Diocesse is not infested with Recusants so dangerousslye as the Bishoprickes of Duresme and Chester, yet in my late Visitacon some have been presented and detected to the number of eightie or thereabouts, and the most of those in some few families, whose Conversion, or reformaion I shall labour both by gentle persuasion and all other good meanes to the utmost of my power.

"Thus in all humilitie and most thankfully acknowledging the happiness wch I enjoy by yor Ma'ties extraordinary benefitts and most gratious favours I shall for ever *ab imo pectore* pray continually for the continuance of yor Ma'ties health and happiness to the Glory of God and the singular comfort of the Christian world.

"Rosecastle August 2, 1617.

> "Yor Ma'ties meanest but most
> "obliged and most dutifull
> "subject and servant
>
> "ROBT. CARLISLE."

Bishop Potter, in a letter to Neile, archbishop of York, reports general conformity in his diocese, but states that the wretched stipends attached to most of the bénefices oblige him to admit mean scholars to the diaconate, rather than allow the people to be utterly without divine service; and he complains much of the supineness of the churchwardens, who never present absentees from church, and of the magistrates, who never punish them.

We quote an account of Carlisle Cathedral in Bishop Potter's time from,—

"A Relation of a short Survey of 26 Counties, &c., observ'd in a seven weekes journey, began at the City of Norwich, and from thence into the North, on Monday, August 11th, 1634, and ending at the same place. By a Captaine, a Lieutenant, and an Ancient, all three of the Military Company in Norwich."

These tourists write as follows :—

"The next day we repayr'd to their Cathedrall, which is nothing so fayre and stately as those we had seene, but more like a great, wild country church: and as it appear'd outwardly so it was inwardly, neither beautify'd nor adorn'd one whit. I remember no more monuments of note, but that of Bishop Oglethorpe, that crowned our late vertuous Queene Elizabeth; and that of Snowden, the Bishop that preach'd Robin Hood to our late renowned King. The organ and voices did well agree, the one being like a shrill bagpipe, the other like the Scottish tone. The sermon, in the like accent, was such as we would hardly bring away, though it was delivered by a neat young scholler (sent that morning from Rose Castle, the Bishop's Mansion, which stands upon Rose and Cawd rivers), one of the Bishop's chaplaines, to supply the Lord's place that day. The Communion also was administred, and receiv'd in a wild and unreverent manner."

No monuments now exist to Oglethorpe and Snowdon. The occasion on which Snowdon preached before the king is commemorated in the following extract from the register of one of the guilds of Carlisle, but how he introduced Robin Hood into his sermon wants elucidation. The following extract from the records of the Merchants' Guild at Carlisle relates to the occasion on which the bishop preached :—

"The King's most excellent majestye, James I., was here at Carliol, the 4 daye of August, 1617, where the Maiore of the city, Mr. Adam Robinson, with Thomas Carleton recorder, and the brethren presentyed hym firste with a speech, then wyth a cup of golde valued at 30*l.* and a purse of sylke, with 40 jacobuses or pieces of the same; his Majestie vouchsafede very pleasantlye the speeche and gyfte, thankyde Mr Maiore, and all the citizens therefore, presentlye wente to the church, accompanyed withe the nobles both of England and Scotland.

The next daye he did keep a feast royall, wentt agayn to the church in state wyth hys nobles, being a saint daye, where preached before hym, Robert Snowdon, bishop of Carliol, and the Maiore that daye going before hym to and from the church att the court gate kyssed his hande att their departure. The thirde daie, the Maiore and the brethren took their leave of hys Majeste who used them very graciouslye."

The bishops of Carlisle with whom we have just been dealing, were, in point of importance, by no means on a footing with their predecessors. It was no longer necessary that bishops of Carlisle should be diplomatists, and commissioners for Scotch affairs, or courtiers or soldiers. Kyte was the last of the diplomatists employed to negotiate for peace with Scotland; Aldridge, or Oglethorpe, the last courtier, and Best, the last bishop of Carlisle that had military custody of Carlisle Castle. With Bishop Barnes began a line of bishops who had nothing to distract them from attending to the diocese of Carlisle, a change which was greatly helped by the union of the two kingdoms. After Barnaby Potter's death, in 1641, the see of Carlisle was given *in commendam* to the celebrated Archbishop Usher, who probably never saw his see, and can have received but little emolument from it.

The deans of Carlisle during this period were Francis White, who succeeded Sir Christopher Perkins in 1622, and became bishop of the see in 1626; Paterson, who held the deanery for three years, until 1629, when he became dean of Exeter; Comber, dean from 1630 until 1642, when he was deprived; these deans have left no mark on the diocese.

During the first thirty or five-and-thirty years of

the seventeenth century, the accounts of the chamberlains of Carlisle show that the mayor and aldermen of that city were on friendly terms with the ecclesiastical dignitaries; the mayor and his brethren dined at Rose Castle and with the dean and prebendaries, and the bishop, the dean, and the prebendaries dined with the mayor and his brethren, and (strange to our notions) on festive occasions accompanied the mayor and his brethren to some hostelry, and there were treated with sack and sherry wines, hot drinks, spices, cakes, and biscuits. Thus:—

"1603. Itm in wine and sugar bestoued upon my Lord bushoppe Robinson. Mr Deputie, and manye other gentlemen when the King was proclaimed. } xxxiiis.

"1614. Upon my lord Carlile (Bishop Robinson) and prebendes a pottle of sack burnt iiis.

"1617. Bestoued in wine and sugar of Mrs Snowden (the new Bishop's wife) at her first coming to Carlell iiijs.

"1621. Wine and sugar that was bestoued upon my Lord Bishop Milburn, at Besse Parkers, Mr Maior and his brethren being present iiijs : vid.

"1624. Itm for wine and sugar which Mr Maior and his bretheren bestoued upon Bishop Sceanouse as a present at his first cominge to the Rose 02 : 18 : 08.

"1627. Itm for wine and sugar bestoued upon the deane (Patterson) 0 : 5 : 6."

The mayor and council attended church regularly, as the following extract from the record of the jury's presentments at the Court Leet held on Monday, October, 1649, shows:—

"We order that (according to an ancient order) the Aldermen of this Citty shall attend the Maior upon every Lord's day to the Church in their gownes and likewise to attend the Maior in the Markett place at or before the Sermon bell to the church sub pena **vis viiid** toties quoties and the Common counsellmen to attend likewise sub pena 3s 4d toties quoties."

From the wording of this order it is clear that the service and the sermon came off at different times. The mayor and his brethren had a "chapel" or pew in St. Mary's; and the officials received an annual payment or fee (as they do now) for laying the cushions, provided by the corporate funds for the greater ease of the civic dignitaries, who also paid for the repair of their "chapel" out of these funds. Occasionally they manifested their appreciation of a sermon by a donation to the preacher.

"1627. Itm a present bestowed upon the deane of winchester the 6th of Maii preaching that same day 0 : 6 : 8.

"Aug 4 1635 bestaued upon Mr Moor preacher in presence of the brethren 0 ·· 2 ·· 8.

"8 Nov 1636 given to a preacher Mr. Porcas 00 : 11 : 00.

"Itm given the 3 Novem to Mr Ogle a blind preacher 0 : 05 : 0.

"Itm to Simond Banks a minister 1 : 6.

"1637. Itm given to a minister called Gray brown the 3 of Julii beinge blind 00 : 02 : 06."

These payments to ministers and preachers do not occur earlier than the dates given; it is probable that the political and theological opinions of some of these preachers would be by no means agreeable to the regular clergy of Carlisle.

CHAPTER IX.

THE TROUBLES, THE RESTORATION, AND THE REVOLUTION.

THE great Civil War commenced in 1642: Charles I. raised his standard at Nottingham on the 23rd of August, and Edgehill was fought on the 23rd of October. For long the tide of battle rolled away from Carlisle, and many persons of distinction sought refuge in it from the perils of war. The battle of Marston Moor was fought on July 1, 1644: York surrendered to the Parliamentary forces on the 16th of that month, and Sir Thomas Glenham, governor of York, and commander-in-chief in the North for the king, took refuge in Cumberland, and after some preliminary skirmishing was locked up in Carlisle, and that city was besieged by David Leslie and a Scotch army. The siege lasted from October, 1644, to June in the following year, and the garrison and inhabitants surrendered through sheer starvation. The victors, in violation of the articles of surrender, played havoc with the cathedral; they pulled down great part of the nave, cloisters, and prebendal houses, and used the materials for the repair of the fortifications. This surrender, indeed, made a clean sweep of everything in Carlisle; bishop, dean, and prebendaries had all been sequestrated and deprived prior to the siege, and disappear, Prebendary West alone surviving to the

Restoration. For two or three years apparently no mayors were elected; certainly no chamberlains of Carlisle kept any accounts: they had no money to account for. When, in 1648-9, we find the accounts resumed, we find the mayor and his brethren established in place of the dean and prebendaries. The mayor and his brethren repaired the two churches; they shifted their chapel or pew from St. Mary's to St. Cuthbert's, where they washed out the royal arms and set up a stand for their sword of honour; they managed the cathedral or grammar school, paid for its repairs, appointed a new master, and paid him out of the tithes of Cargo, which they had become possessed of: they turned the deanery into a poorhouse; and they kept a register in their great "Dormant Book" of the sales of the sequestrated episcopal and capitular estates.

The Solemn League and Covenant of 1643 had ejected several of the Episcopalian clergy of the diocese, and some that remained were ejected on the "Vacancy of Ministers" in 1655. The two churches of St. Mary and St. Cuthbert, Carlisle, became thus vacant; the mayor and his brethren held a great competitive preaching, which lasted from December in that year until the following May, when they appointed Mr. Timothy Tullie and Mr. Comfort Starr. The competitors included some eminent lights of Nonconformity, the Rev. George Larkham, known as "the Star of the North;" the Rev. Richard Gilpin; and the Rev. Nathaniel Burnand. Tullie also held a lectureship at St. Cuthbert's Church, whose stipend the mayor and his brethren partly paid; the lectureship can be traced back in the chamberlain's accounts and municipal records to 1625; it was probably founded under the order of Queen Elizabeth appointing lecturers in cathedrals, and removed from the cathedral to St. Cuthbert when the nave was pulled down.[1]

We shall presently return to the doings in the cathedral and city of Carlisle: we must now direct our attention to a remote corner of the diocese as extended in 1856. In 1652, George Fox was travelling in the Yorkshire dales: he visited the annual hiring fair held at Sedbergh, and preached in the churchyard; a disturbance took place, an attempt was made to put him down, and one Francis Howgill, an Independent minister, took part with Fox, and procured him a hearing. Next Sunday, Francis Howgill, and one John Audland, also an Independent minister, and both afterwards energetic ministers among the Friends, were preaching in Firbank Chapel, in Westmorland, a place now included in the extended diocese of Carlisle. To this place came George Fox, and, in the afternoon, after people had had their dinners, he addressed a congregation of about a thousand in number, from a rock which was close to the chapel, so close, indeed,

---

[1] See Lectureships at St. Cuthbert's, Carlisle,—*Transactions Cumberland and Westmorland Archæological Society*, vol. vi. p. 312. Was this lecturer the *Theologic Prelector*, newly-appointed in 1571, whom Bishop Barnes charged to preach on certain occasions? See "Visitations in the Ancient Diocese of Carlisle," Dr. Prescott, p. 36, *n*. There was also a cathedral lecturer from 1684 to 1855.

that many of the elders listened to him from the chapel windows; while he explained to them that he preached from the rock rather than in the chapel, because, in his opinion, no more sanctity appertained to the one than to the other. The result of this meeting at Firbank, famous in the annals of the Society of Friends, was that he obtained many followers, including both Howgill and Audland, who became the earliest and most ardent missionaries of the Society. From Firbank, Fox proceeded by Preston Patrick to Kendal, where he held a meeting in the Town Hall. He next went to Underbarrow and Crook, at which places he had great success. He then returned to Lancashire, but frequently during the year visited Westmorland. From that county and North Lancashire he collected the first missionaries of the Society, namely, Edward Burrough, John Audland, Francis Howgill, John Camm, George Whitehead, Richard Hubberthorne, Thomas Holmes, Miles Halhead, and Miles Hubbersty, the majority of whom were Westmorland men. Fox numbered also among his local friends and followers two men of official position, namely, Gervaise Benson and Anthony Pearson: the first was justice for Cumberland and Westmorland, and the second for both these counties and Lancashire as well. Both were converted and both wrote books, one against tithes, the other against oaths. In the following year, 1653, Fox was informed that the people in Cumberland had vowed to take his life if he put foot in that county. Fox was in no way deterred by this, but joined Justice Pearson and his wife, who were on their way to Carlisle Quarter Sessions. Fox only accompanied them as far as Bootle, where he presented himself at church on Sunday, and so soon as the priest had finished preaching he commenced, according to the custom of the time, a discourse of his own. Two sermons in such rapid succession were more than the people would stand, or else the priest incited them to violence, though it was then usual for any minister of any religious society to preach and officiate in a parish church after the hours of regular service. They pulled Fox out into the churchyard, and, spite of the constable's exertions, beat him severely, nearly breaking his wrist. Nothing daunted by this rough treatment, Fox returned in the afternoon to the churchyard, and seated himself upon a cross there, while some of his comrades entered the church, where they found a stranger from London officiating. They beckoned Fox in, and, spite of the priest from London, he succeeded in preaching, being protected by the constable. Fox stayed some days at "Milholm in Bootel," and from thence went to make an appointment with Priest Wilkinson, who had three churches near Cockermouth, Brigham, and (probably) Mosser Chapel and Greysouthen. At one of these churches (name not given) the concourse of people anxious to hear Fox was so great that the place resembled a fair, and his audience included a party of twelve soldiers and their wives, from the Cromwellian garrison of Carlisle, Priest Larkham (the Star of the North), and others. Both here and at Brigham, Fox had a more friendly reception than at Bootle:

the people welcomed him into the church, where he preached, the effects of which Wilkinson immediately tried to counteract by a sermon of several hours in length. Fox gained the day, and convinced many, including the twelve soldiers, who went with him to Cockermouth, protected him, and hindered those who wished to prevent him from preaching in the church of that town. Preach he did, "largely," as his journal expresses it. By Caldbeck and the Borders Fox passed to Carlisle, where the Baptists and their minister met him, and held a meeting in the abbey. Fox quaintly describes the pastor of the Carlisle Baptists as—

"An high notionist and a flashy man, who came to me and asked me what must be damned. I was moved immediately to tell him that which spake in him was to be damned; this stopped the pastor's mouth."

From the abbey, Fox went to the castle; the garrison was at once assembled by tuck of drum to hear him preach. Some of the sergeants, however, demurred, not to his preaching, but to his doctrine. On the market-day, Fox preached in the market-place, and all passed off peaceably, spite of threats by the magistrates. On Sunday, he went to the "Steeple House," evidently the cathedral. There he attempted to preach. A riot ensued,—soldiers, magistrates' wives, and mob, all fighting with sticks and stones, and yelling, "Down with the Roundheads" until at last the governor of the castle appeared with several files of musketeers, cleared the place, and arrested some of the rioters. Fox escaped by connivance of the military. Next day he was brought before the justices of the city, who were all Presbyterians and Independents; they committed him to prison "as a blasphemer, an heretic, and a seducer." There he was to remain until the assizes, and the report was that he was to be hanged. A flaw was discovered in the order of commitment, and Fox was not put upon trial at the assizes, but was detained in close confinement. His friends, Benson and Pearson, strenuously moved for his freedom. They circulated letters and broadsheets, and at their instigation Parliament took up the matter, and instituted an inquiry. Fox was set free and his gaolers punished. Fox did not immediately leave Cumberland; he went to Caldbeck, where the people beat his comrades; to Wigton, where the people formed a guard armed with pitchforks, and would let no Quaker enter the town; to Gilsland, where he was taken for a horse-stealer; and, finally, to Uldale where he addressed a meeting of many thousand people. Fox, in this visit to the two counties, got a large number of converts, including several soldiers, who were shortly discharged from the Parliamentary forces, because they would not take an oath of allegiance to Cromwell. Fox revisited the two counties in 1657 and 1663, on each occasion narrowly escaping arrest. We have no records of any further visits; but the number of early preachers of his theology that came from Westmorland and Cumberland, and from North Lancashire, and the number of Friends there, show how deeply his teaching must have taken root. Plenty of evidence can be obtained from " the

Papers of Mr. Secretary Williamson," of which a calendar is in the Rolls Series, as to the growth of the Society. In November, 1663, Sir Daniel Fleming, a prominent Westmorland magistrate, writes to Williamson :—

"If mischief arise now, it will be from non-licensed ministers or from Quakers, of whom there are too many in the part of the county joining to Lancashire, where George Fox and most of his cults have been long kennelled. They keep weekly meetings within eight miles of each other through all this country, if not through England : they will do mischief most resolutely if Fox, or any other of their grand speakers, dictate it ; and some threaten already."

Sir Philip Musgrave, a Cumberland justice, writes :—

"The Quakers grow bold enough to meet two hundred or more at a time ; they keep copies of proceedings against them by justices of the peace, to be ready against a time when they shall call the justices to account."

The justices passed away before they could be called to account, but Besse, in his huge folio volumes, has published in minute detail the memoranda thus kept. It should be said that Fleming and Musgrave lumped together all Nonconformists as fanatics and Quakers.[1]

The Restoration found only one of the sequestrated dignitaries of the see still living, Lewis West, prebendary of the third stall in Carlisle Cathedral. The bishopric of Carlisle was offered to Dr. Richard

[1] The above account of Fox is (abbreviated) from "Early Cumberland and Westmorland Friends," by the writer of this book.

Gilpin, rector of Greystoke, who declined the offer, not on account of any invincible objection to episcopacy, but because he could by no means be wrought upon to sign the Solemn League and Covenant. Finally, Richard Sterne, the deprived master of Jesus College, Cambridge, was appointed to the see: he was translated to York in 1664. Guy Carleton, a local man, educated at Carlisle Grammar School and at Queen's, Oxford, an exile to the Continent for his loyalty, was made dean, and held that preferment until, in 1671, he was made Bishop of Bristol, from which see he was translated to Chichester in 1685. To the vacant stalls in the cathedral, Thomas Canon, Arthur Savage, and George Buchanan were appointed, of whom Savage had been ejected from the living of Bromfield, and Buchanan from Kirkby Lonsdale. Two munificent prelates followed, Edward Rainbow, 1665 to 1684, and Thomas Smith, 1684 to 1702. Munificence, indeed, was necessary in bishops and deans of Carlisle, for the Restoration found the episcopal palace of Rose, the deanery, the prebendal houses, and the nave of the cathedral mere ruins. Bishop Sterne rebuilt the chapel at Rose, but so badly that Bishop Rainbow had again to rebuild it; and Bishop Smith (while dean) rebuilt the deanery, in addition to giving an organ and communion plate to the cathedral. As bishop, he built largely at Rose, and other places in the diocese benefited by his liberality.

A most amiable picture of Bishop Rainbow is given in a short life of him published in 1688. It also contains his funeral sermon, which was preached by his chancellor and chaplain, Thomas Tullie, afterwards dean of Carlisle. Edward Rainbow was born at Bliton, in Lincolnshire, of which place his father was rector, a man noted for his learning and virtue; his mother was also skilled in the Latin, Greek, and Hebrew languages. After being a short time at school at Gainsborough, young Rainbow was sent to Dr. John Williams's, at Peterborough; he was removed thence to Westminster School, on Dr. Williams being appointed dean of Westminster and bishop of Lincoln. From Westminster he proceeded to Oxford, but two years later he migrated to Magdalen College, Cambridge, induced thereto by being nominated to a scholarship in the patronage of the Countess of Warwick. He became a fellow of that college, and attained distinction at the university as a preacher; ultimately he became master of his college, but was ejected from that post by the Rump Parliament, and retired to a small country living. On the Restoration he returned to his old post at Magdalen, and was shortly appointed dean of Peterborough. These appointments he gave up on being appointed in 1665 to the see of Carlisle, though he might have retained one or other for some time *in commendam* with his bishopric. It is characteristic of the man, that when thus giving up a secure income, he had to borrow money to defray the charges of his consecration, first-fruits, and his journey to and settlement in his diocese, where the ruined state of Rose Castle involved him in a heavy outlay on building, and in a protracted litigation about dilapidations with his predecessor and metropolitan

Sterne. Rainbow's biographer is very reticent about names and cases, but it is clear Rainbow found much in his diocese that required to be reformed; negligent and immoral clergy, who did not hesitate, when rebuked, to publicly affront their bishop. He appears to have been outspoken generally in the denunciation of immorality, and to have so offended some great lady about the Court, once a friend of his, who revenged herself by preventing his translation to Lincoln. He was very earnest in impressing upon his clergy, by his example as well as by precept, the diligent preaching of God's word, the due administration of the holy sacraments, and the catechising of youth. So long as his health would allow he preached frequently in his cathedral, in his chapel at Rose, in Dalston church, and in the churches and chapels in the vicinity. His liberality was unbounded. In dear years, when his own stores were exhausted, he bought barley and distributed it to the poor, sometimes as many as seven or eight score being relieved in one day by the porter at Rose. To the poor at Carlisle and at Dalston he made regular allowances. He paid for the education of poor boys at Dalston school, and for putting them out as apprentices; he supported poor scholars at the universities; he subscribed largely to the French Protestants and to foreign converts. Much of this was done in secret, even without the knowledge of his wife, who was a worthy helpmate to the good bishop. His domestic life was most exemplary; four times a day he assembled his family for divine worship, twice in the chapel, when a chaplain officiated, and twice in the dining-room, at 6 a.m. and 9 p.m., when his lordship officiated. His biographer says of his house :—

"All known Profaness and Swearing were banished thence: For this made as much discord in that Family, as an ill Musician did in *Plato's* Schools. Offenders in Debauchery were at first reproved and admonish d; and if they relapsed into the same Fault, they were often dismiss'd the House; unless there appeared visible signs of Repentance, and those ushered in with fervent Promises, to make those good by their utmost endeavours. .... Neither was his Hospitality offending against the Canons of the Church; but like that of a Bishop. His Entertainment was free: his Table was well furnished with Varieties; his Conversation pleasant and yet grave, divertive and yet instructing; often feeding the Minds, as well as the bodies of his Guests."

The good prelate died in 1684, and was buried, by his own request, not in his cathedral but at Dalston, under a plain stone, with the simple inscription :—

"Depositum Edvardi Rainbow
Epis. Carliol. Obijt Vices$^{mo.}$
Sexto die Martij M.DC.LXXXIV."

Scholar though he was, Rainbow left no works in print but three occasional sermons, one of which he preached at the funeral at Appleby of Anne, Countess of Pembroke, Dorset, and Montgomery, in 1676. These sermons are now very scarce. The mode of life of this excellent prelate must have been in striking contrast to that of many in his diocese, if Macaulay's sketch of a seventeenth-century squire is a true one.

Rainbow's successor, Thomas Smith, was born in the parish of Asby, in Westmorland, and went from Appleby grammar school to Queen's College, Oxford, where he became fellow, and a celebrated tutor. During the civil wars he retired to the north; on the Restoration he was appointed chaplain to the king, and prebendary of Durham. In 1671 he became dean of Carlisle, and rebuilt the deanery, which dean Carleton had left in the ruins he found it in after the civil wars. In 1684 Smith, then in his seventieth year, was appointed bishop of Carlisle. He found a young and active archdeacon of twenty-nine years, left him by his predecessor, in the famous William Nicolson, and throughout his episcopate archdeacon Nicolson was a leading spirit in the diocese. We shall have much to say of Nicolson when we come to his appointment as bishop of Carlisle. Bishop Smith's enthronement in his cathedral was conducted with much ceremony; the mayor and corporation and the leading citizens went out of Carlisle as far as Brisco, to meet the new prelate, who had spent the previous night at Hutton-ith-Forest, the seat of Sir George Fletcher, M.P. At the market-cross he was met by the clergy, the cathedral dignitaries and the singing-men, and conducted to the cathedral and the chapter-house, where the necessary ceremonies were duly observed, after which the great men of the party were entertained in the deanery by the new dean, Dr. Thomas Musgrave. There is little to tell about Smith's episcopate, which terminated with his death in 1702, but the list of his expenditure on public objects:—

Building the deanery at Carlisle	£600
Organ at Carlisle, £220, communion plate, £100	320
Prebendal house at Carlisle	50
Altering house and building stables at Rose	300
New tower there and court walls	167
School at Dalston, £30, tenement there, £80	110
Court-house at Dalston	50
Library and Register's office at Carlisle	120
To the Dean and Chapter	100
Pigeon-cote at Rose	53
To the several parishes in his diocese by his will	230
School at Carlisle	500
Vicarage of Penrith	500
Vicarage of Dalston	300
The school and master's house at Appleby, and cloisters there	626
The poor and school at Asby	100
Towards building St. Paul's	150
New library at Queen's College	100
More to the said college	500
Other colleges and chapels	50
Prebendal house at Durham, and organ	300
Total	**£5,226**

The total is a very large sum of money, for days in which a squire with £400 a year was thought a well-to-do man.

To return to the Restoration; that event was speedily followed by the Act of Uniformity, under which, on St. Bartholomew Day, 1662, about a fifth of the English clergy were driven from their parishes as Nonconformists. About twenty-four of the Cromwellian ministers in Cumberland, and five or six in Westmorland refused to conform. Some of these, like Dr. Gilpin, of Greystoke; Benson, of Bridekirk;

Baldwin, of Penrith; and Comfort Starr, of Carlisle, left the district; others, like Burnand, of Brampton, and Larkham, of Cockermouth, remained and exercised their gifts in private, unsilenced by the Conventicle Act of 1664. After a time of persecution, Charles II., in 1672, issued the "Declaration of Indulgence," enacting that, upon application a person could obtain a licence to preach, the same favour being granted to certain houses, rooms, barns, or buildings to be used for preaching therein. Mr. Blair, F.S.A., has kindly furnished me with the following list of those registered for Cumberland [1]:—

"The house of George Larkham at Hameshill in the parish of Bride-Kirke Cumb^d 8 May 1672

"License to George Larkham to be a Pr teacher in his house in Hameshill in the parish of Bridekirk Cumb^d 8 May 1672

"The house of John Noble in Graestoke Cumberland Pr

"License to Anty Sleigh to be a Pr Teacher in the house of John Noble in Graestoke Cumb^d

"License to John Davy to be a Cong^l Teacher in Reginald Waltons house at Aulston More Cumb^d 29 June 1672

"The house of Reginald Walton at Alston More in Cumb^d Cong^l 29 June.

"The house of George Larkham in Bridekirk Cumb^d Pr 16 July.

"License for the house of Garwen Wrean at Crosthwaite Cumb^d July 16

"The Like for Richd Lowreys house at Cockermouth Cumb^d 16 July

"Like for Richd Egleshold's house at Allarby Cumb^d 16 July

---

[1] See "Archæologia Æliana," vol. xiii. pp. 33 and 63. They are taken from "The Domestic Entry Book of Charles II.," in the Record Office.

"Like for Thomas Younghusbands house at Torpenhow Cumb^d 16 July

"License to Giles Nicholson of Kirkheswold Cumberland July 22

"The house of Natha: Burnan, of Branton in Cumberland, to be a Pr teacher Sept 5

"The house of Wm Jameson of Kirkoswold Cumberland Pr

"The house of Wm Atkinson of Brampton in Cumberland Pr

"Like for the house of John Carse at Embleton Cumb^d 16 July
Sept 5

"The house of Gowdon Wreen of Crosthwaite in Cumb^d Cong^l Sep^t 5

"The house of Edw James of Blackfryers in Carlisle in Cumberland Pr

"The house of — Wilson at Crosfield in Cumb^d

"The house of Thos Thorkold of Kirkoswold Cumb^d Pr

"The house of Thos^s Langhome of Penrick in Cumb^d Cong^l

"License to Gawin Eaglesfield Indp^t teacher at his own house at Dearlam in Cumberland

"The house of Isabella Dixon of Whitehaven in Cumb^d Indp^t

"The house of Thos Barnes of Holmcaltram in Cumberland Indp^t

Of these, Gawen Wren was a Quaker, the only one; George Larkham, registered as a Presbyterian, was an Independent; Natha. Burnan is Nathaniel Burnand, the ejected vicar of Brampton, and brother-in-law of Dr. Richard Gilpin, whose house, Scaleby Castle, in Cumberland, is also licensed, but has got by mistake into the Northumberland list, no doubt because Gilpin himself was minister of the Presbyterian chapel at Newcastle in 1672. Gilpin, Presbyterian, and Larkham, Independent, were the two great apostles of local seventeenth-century nonconformity, and the other persons named, except Wren, would be disciples of one or other of them; we fancy all the older nonconformist bodies in the diocese can trace a pedigree to one or other of these two ministers. The licences were very soon withdrawn, and persecution recommenced, as the records of the Quarter Sessions show, where, however, the majority of the persons proceeded against were Quakers, though the justices seem to have had fits of severity against Papists alternating with those against Quakers: thus in 1674 the offenders were chiefly Quakers of the yeomen and humbler classes; in 1680 they were chiefly Papists, and of the squirearchy.

Charles II. had at least one sincere admirer among the higher clergy of the diocese of Carlisle. Archdeacon (afterwards bishop) Nicolson, in his diary,[1] under "11 Feb., 1684" (the archdeacon keeps his diary by the ecclesiastical and not the historical year), writes:—

"The ill news of ye Death of Charles ye Second: Regum Optimi."

Charles had indeed been very gracious to the archdeacon on his being presented to him at Windsor in that year.

The archdeacon took an active part in procuring signatures to an address to the new king; rival drafts of this were prepared by the bishop, Dr. Smith, and

[1] Several volumes of the diaries of this active prelate are in existence, and there is reason to hope they may shortly be made public. At present the writer has only seen one,— that for 1684-5.

by the dean, Dr. Musgrave, but it is not clear which was adopted; probably the bishop's, as Nicolson, who was his right hand, took charge of it, got the signatures of the prebendaries, and then travelled up and down the diocese to obtain signatures from the clergy [1]; he records a convivial evening spent during the trip with the chancellor, Thomas Tullie, at which the toast of "Prosperity to ye Church of England in Spight of Popery and Fanaticism" was drunk.

James II. filled the Corporation of Carlisle with partisans of his own, as indeed he did every post that he could: Carlisle he garrisoned with a regiment of Irish Papists, whose doings are thus recorded :—

"This was in the Year 1688, about which Time came the News of the Queen's being with Child; and the Papists, being greatly overjoyed thereat, made Bone-fires in the Market-place, and, in a publick, exalted, and triumphant Manner, drank Healths to the young Prince: And I being a Spectator, with many other young Men of the Town, the Officers called several of us to drink the Health with them; and then I took occasion to ask one of the Captains how they knew the Child would be a Prince; might it not happen to be a Princess? No,

---

[1] Thomas Story, the eminent Quaker, Recorder of Pennsylvania, and the friend of Penn, says :—"In this Conjunctors, the whole Protestant Parts of the King's Dominions, were in great Consternation, and apprehensive of a Popish Government, and consequent Oppression, and Persecution to Destruction. Nevertheless, whether out of Fear, or other cause, as well the Bishops as inferior Clergy, and the generality of the People throughout the King's Dominions, presented addresses to him . . . replete with the utmost expressions of Loyalty and Duty that words were capable of."—*Story's Journal*, p. 7.

replied he, sir, that cannot be, for this Child comes by the Prayers of the Church ; the Church has prayed for a Prince, and it can be no otherwise. And, when the News came of his Birth, they made another great Fire in the same Place ; when they drank Wine, till, with that, and the Transport of the News, they were exceedingly distracted, throwing their Hats into the Fire at one Health, their Coats at the next, their Waistcoats at a third, and so on to their Shoes ; and some of them threw in their Shirts, and then ran about naked, like Madmen."—*Story's Journal*, p. 7.

In the diocese of Carlisle the Revolution of 1688 was, in spite of these heroics, effected with great quietness : Lowther, of Whitehaven, secured the seaports for William III., and the Irish Papists that garrisoned Carlisle got over the walls and ran away by night, and the stout-hearted sheriff, William Stanley, proclaimed William III. and Mary at the market-cross.

The clergy in the diocese of Carlisle, or some of them, were evidently uneasy about their duty under the new state of things, and in May 1689 Archdeacon Nicolson addressed a circular letter to the clergy in his archdeaconry. In it (it is too long to reproduce at length) he urges the necessity of the clergy being unanimous among themselves, particularly in times when all sorts of rumours were flying about,—rumours of revolt in the army, of invasions by Popish Highlanders, rumours that all the parsons were only waiting a favourable moment to declare for King James, and such like stories,—all which tended to alienate the parsons' friends, and to provoke their enemies,

"upon the first popular insurrection to fall on us, as abettors of Idolatry and traitors to our own establishment. And it must be confessed that some of the more unwarily scrupulous among us have given too great encouragement to these wicked attempts. I am glad to find us so generally concerned to preserve and keep close to our antient principles of loyalty, which have hitherto been the glory of our Church; and may they for ever continue to be so. But to live answerably in our practices requires a deal of unprejudiced reasoning and circumspection in some junctures, lest we misplace our obedience; and, out of a true design to approve ourselves most steadily loyal, fall into the very dregs of treason and rebellion. We have now a Prince and Princess seated on the English throne, in whom we are ready enough to acknowledge all the accomplishments that we can wish for in our governors, provided their title to the present possession of the Crown were unquestionable; and, therefore, methinks we should rather greedily catch at any appearance of proof that may justify their pretensions, than dwell upon such arguments as seemingly overturn them."

The archdeacon then proceeds to discuss various questions with the view of showing that William III. was king *de jure* as well as *de facto;* he deals with the effect of the late king's desertion of his government, and the action taken by the Convention. He says:—

"The short of our case is the late king was pleased unexpectedly to leave us; and their present Majesties have stepped into the throne as the next lawful successors. And where is the mischief of all this? You and I are not yet called upon to give our assent to every vote that passed in either House of Parliament in the management of this matter, and I hope we never shall. But I think we ought thankfully to join in the last result of their councils that William and Mary, Prince and Princess of Orange, are honestly and legally seated on the English throne. And this may be done without an unnecessary acquainting the world with our opinion whether the royal dignity has devolved upon them by right of succession or they have attained it by a new grant from the people."

Nicolson then examines at length the popular objections to this doctrine,—viz., the want of a proper inquiry into the birth of the Prince of Wales; the doctrine of passive obedience in face of James's rumoured league with the French king for the destruction of Protestants; and the example of Sancroft, archbishop of Canterbury, who had declined to take the oaths of allegiance to William and Mary, on which Nicolson remarks that the clergy here should have regard rather to the behaviour of their own metropolitan and diocesan than to that of his Grace of Canterbury. He concludes:—

"In short, sir, we have the judgment of a vast majority of both the Divines and Lawyers of the kingdom that a firm allegiance is due to their present Majesties, King William and Queen Mary. And the pressing necessities of our Church call for a speedy resolution of letting the world know (to the astonishment of our enemies and comfort of our friends) that we are heartily of the same opinion.

"I am, yours, &c.,
"W. N."

No record has come to our knowledgment of the reception this letter met with, or the effect it had, but Archbishop Sancroft and eight of his episcopal brethren absolutely refused to take the oath to the new sovereign; their example was followed by about four hundred clergymen, who became known by the name of "Non-jurors."

Towards the close of the seventeenth century public attention was directed to the alarming increase of coarseness and immorality throughout the kingdom. It soon became the subject of a Royal proclamation, which was ultimately embodied in an Act of Parliament. The religious world was roused to the evil, and *societies for the suppressing of immorality and profaneness* sprang up in almost every county, but principally in London, to check by united effort, the prevailing sin. Books and pamphlets were written, explaining the object of the crusade, and calling upon Churchmen and Dissenters alike to join in it. In the city of Carlisle, the moving spirit in establishing in 1699 a branch of "the Society for the Reformation of Manners" was the recorder, William Gilpin, son of the celebrated Richard Gilpin, of Scaleby Castle and Newcastle, the *quondam* rector of Greystoke, and Presbyterian minister; the patronage of the aged Bishop of Carlisle, Dr. Smith, was secured by a surprise, and matters looked like a success. But Archdeacon Nicolson made strenuous opposition. He took his stand on the Canons, which he alleged, were binding on his conscience, and denounced those clergy who ignored them by joining in "conventicles" with dissenting ministers under cover of furthering the interests of morals, while in reality they were causing schism and breaking the law.

"You may probably have heard of a society, league, or covenant at Carlisle, wherein the Churchmen and Dissenters are mutually engaged for the Reformation of manners. We certainly are all obliged to prosecute the good ends of his Majesty's late proclamation in our several stations; but give me leave to tell you that our zeal for the service of Religion ought to be regulated by the laws of the land and Canons of the Church. We must beware of making ourselves parties to conventicles and unlawful assemblies, by meeting in numbers (above five besides our own families) on a religious account, unless we can secure ourselves of the benefit of the Act of Toleration; and (then) we are Dissenters and not members of the Established Church. If we desire to continue in our present Communion we ought well to consider the words and meaning of the twelfth Canon."¹

The clergy, as a whole, were willing enough to follow their archdeacon's advice, till Chancellor Tullie ranged himself on the other side and went in strongly for the amalgamation of Church and Dissent. Under his ægis Cockburn, the vicar of Brampton, aided by a few of the neighbouring clergy, set up a society at Brampton, a place where Gilpin possessed considerable influence. Here arrangements were made for a weekly lecture at which Cockburn, two other neighbouring vicars, and a dissenting minister were to preside in turn. This soon brought down the archdeacon's thunders on Cockburn's head. Nicolson thus reasons with him—

"The reformation of manners is a most Christian duty, and we are under an indispensable obligation to endeavour it, according to the King's late excellent proclamation, by the most effectual means allowed and prescribed by law. I fear these societies are not legal ways of procedure. I am confident you will be of my mind, when you have carefully perused the twelfth Canon. The censure there denounced is a terrible one; and wise men will beware of doing anything that does so much as look like the anabaptistical error which is there condemned."²

---

¹ "Letters on Various Subjects, &c., to and from Bishop Nicolson." London: John Nichols & Son, 1809. Letter to Mr. Gregory, p. 151.

² *Ibid.*, Letter to Mr. Cockburn, p. 145.

Archdeacon and chancellor were summoned to Rose Castle to answer to their aged diocesan for the strife they were causing in his diocese. Little came out of it. The bishop was too old and too infirm to curb the enterprising zeal of his ecclesiastical subordinates. An appeal was made to the Archbishop of York, but he shelved the question; the Bishop of Chester was inclined to side with Chancellor Tullie, but finally the Bishop of Carlisle drew up the following paper to be dispersed among his diocese:—

"I. I earnestly desire all my Clergy zealously to promote the good ends of his Majesty's late proclamation; not only by their frequent Sermons on that subject, but likewise by such voluntary meetings and conferences amongst themselves (weekly or monthly) as may most conveniently be had, or such other methods (allowed by the Canons of the Church and the Laws of the Land) as they shall occasionally agree on.

"II. That in these conferences and meetings they would (as they see it necessary) request the company and assistance of such neighbouring Justices of the Peace, and other persons of note and gravity, as may best forward these their good designs.

"III. That, in their said consults, they confer only with such persons as are well affected to the doctrine and discipline of the Established Church." [1]

The following presentment by churchwardens was extracted by Mr. W. Jackson, F.S.A., from the duplicate Scaleby Registers in the Bishop's Registry at Carlisle:—

"The presentment of the parish of Scalby [Scaleby] An. Dom. 1684.

---

[1] *Ibid.*, Letter to Archbishop of York, p. 163. The whole correspondence is in "Letters to and from Bishop Nicolson," and is most interesting.

Impr'im. To the first Article of the Title of the book of Visitation exhibited at the Bishop's last triennial Visitation we answer that our Church is so far from being in good repair that it is no wise fit for the publick worship of God.

2ndly. We have no carpet cloath Surplice or pulpit cloath.

3rd. We have noe Church Bible book of Homilies or other books required by the Canons of our Church.

4ly. Wee know off noe Church Stock or poore stock belonging to our parish nor can Devine how the same hath been Raised or disposed of.

To the first article of the second Title.

1st. Wee answer that our Churchyard is not sufficiently fenced from Annoyances.

2nd. The dwelling house and outhouses belonging to our Minister are wholey gone to decay and Ruine and that they have been so this many years.

3rd. Wee have noe Terrier off of the glebe Lands belonging nor can we learn how the same hath been lost.

To the fourth Title.

1st. Wee answer that we have in our parish severall separatists viz John Pearson of Stoneknowe quaker, William Gash, John Scot of Highberries, John Goodfellow of Scaleby Hill.

2ndly. We have in our parish found to be guilty of adulterie (three couples). Noe register book."

It must not be assumed that Scaleby was a representative seventeenth-century parish in the diocese of Carlisle; its proximity to the Borders caused it to fall a ready prey to Scottish invaders. In 1703 Bishop Nicolson commends the fabric of the church, so that it must have been restored; but there was no font, no altar-rail, no surplice, or Common Prayer-book.

The following account of Carlisle cathedral at the end of the seventeenth century (1687) is interesting, though well known locally. Tradition says that

Carlisle cathedral is the only cathedral in England that has never had candlesticks on the altar since the Reformation: copes were worn in it by Gospeller and Epistoler as late as 1778.

"About this Time I went diligently to the publick Worship, especially to the Cathedral at Carlisle; where in time of publick Prayer, we used all (Male and Female) as soon as that Creed, call it the *Apostles' Creed*, began to be said, to turn our Faces towards the East; and, when the word JESUS was mentioned, we all, as one, bowed and kneeled towards the Altar-table, as they call it, where stood a Couple of Common Prayer Books, in Folio, one at each Side of the Table, and over them, painted upon the Wall H.S. signifying JESUS, *Hominum Salvator.*"
—*Story's Journal.*

CHAPTER X.

THE EIGHTEENTH CENTURY.

THE first Bishop of Carlisle in the eighteenth century was the celebrated, learned, and very busy prelate, William Nicolson,[1] 1702 to 1718. He was the son of the Rev. Joseph Nicolson, who was ejected from Plumbland in Cumberland by Cromwell's Commissioners, but who lived to be restored; and the bishop's mother was a Brisco, of Crofton, whence he must have inherited a strong Puritan strain. He was sent to Oxford, and there he found a patron in Sir Joseph William, Secretary of State, son of a former vicar of Bridekirk, and by him he was sent to Leipsic in 1678 to study foreign languages, and in the following year he travelled in France. He took to literary work and published a huge atlas in several volumes. In 1681 Bishop Rainbow appointed him to a stall in Carlisle cathedral, with the vicarage of Torpenhow, and in 1682 to the archdeaconry of Carlisle, which was held with the rectory of Great Salkeld. He immediately devoted his energies to deciphering the runic inscriptions in the diocese, and to the study of its natural history and antiquities. In 1696, 1697, and 1698, he

---

[1] See *ante*, p. 154, for a note as to the diaries kept by this bishop.

published the three parts of his "English Historical Libraries"; he published a similar work for Scotland in 1702, and one for Ireland at a much later period. As the county histories say, this publication involved him in many controversies. We shall see the truth of this.

In 1702 Nicolson was appointed Bishop of Carlisle, and was consecrated at Lambeth in June. He was, no doubt, as an active archdeacon and a beneficed clergyman in the diocese, well acquainted with its condition. But he lost no time in making a thorough investigation into the same. In 1703 he commenced his primary visitation; in addition to summoning his clergy to meet him at various convenient centres, he went himself to every church in the diocese, personally inspected its condition, made notes thereon, and copied all the inscriptions to be found. These notes have recently been published by the Cumberland and Westmorland Archæological Society, under the title of "Miscellany Accounts of the Diocese of Carlisle, with the Terriers delivered into me at my Primary Visitation, by William Nicolson, late Bishop of Carlisle." The book gives a curious and minute, but most deplorable picture of the diocese. The fabrics of the churches, especially of the impropriated chancels, were commonly in a very bad condition,— other things were to match. Frequently no Bible of the modern version, though that was then over a hundred years old; no prayer-book, no surplice, no altar-rails; in some cases the table stood east and west. Education neglected almost everywhere, though the church was too commonly the only school-house.

The clergy were miserably poor, and shamefully robbed by the lay impropriators. Occasionally scandalous churches were matched by scandalous vicars. It must have taxed all Nicolson's energies to effect an improvement, but we shall see that it was done, though not perhaps always in his time.

Nicolson soon found himself with other work on hand of a troublesome character; he had, in his "English Historical Library," dealt roughly with some little works by Dr. Todd, a canon of Carlisle; the celebrated Dr. Atterbury had severely criticised the "English Historical Library," and to him Nicolson had replied.

In the year 1704, the then Dean of Carlisle, Dr. Graham, a member of the Netherby family, was appointed and duly installed as Dean of Wells. The deanery of Carlisle was given to Dr. Atterbury, a somewhat unfortunate appointment, considering the ill-feeling known to exist between him and Bishop Nicolson. The patent under the broad seal commanded the admission of Dr. Atterbury to the deanery of Carlisle then vacant *sive per cessionem sive per resignationem*. A difficulty was raised, whether by Nicolson or not does not appear, on the point that Graham's installation at Wells did not vacate the deanery of Carlisle, and Dr. Atterbury, as a precaution, possessed himself of a written resignation by Dr. Graham of that deanery. In September, 1704, the new dean started to go to Carlisle to be installed. At Bishopsthorpe he found a communication from the Bishop of Carlisle, enclosing a form of retractation which the bishop required Dr. Atterbury to sign as a condition precedent to his installation as Dean of Carlisle. The form ran thus:—

"1. The Queen of England out of Parliament has not the same authority in causes ecclesiastical that the Christian emperors had in the Primitive Church.

2. The Church of England is under two sovereigns; the one absolute and the other limited.

3. The supreme ecclesiastical jurisdiction, as annexed to the Imperial Crown of this realm, can be exercised no otherwise than in Parliament.

These three propositions, separating her Majesty's authority from her person, and impeaching her legal supremacy, are erroneous, and contrary to the received doctrine of the Church of England, as well as the known laws of the realm. And therefore (so far as they or any of them are deducible from anything that I have heretofore asserted and published) I do hereby, openly and freely, revoke and renounce the same."

Accompanying this form of retractation, was a request from Nicolson to the Archbishop of York, asking him to give Atterbury institution by his metropolitic authority, in the event of Atterbury declining to sign. Atterbury of course declined to sign, and the Archbishop of York, who seems to have been most anxious to make peace, wrote to the Bishop of Carlisle, asking that prelate to send a commission, under seal, authorising the archbishop, or some commissioners, whose names he suggested, to institute, as he was advised he could not institute without. Nicolson replied that he would give a commission under his seal to nobody, for doing anything which he would not and could not do himself, and therefore Atterbury must come to him. Dr. Atterbury, therefore, attended at Rose, when he found that the bishop had, on the advice of the archbishop, withdrawn the form of retractation just mentioned. But he had prepared another, which he required Atterbury to sign. Atterbury replied by a written protest and demand for institution, and declined to discuss the matter further. The bishop then demanded Atterbury's orders and letters testimonial of his good life and behaviour, and then proposed to examine him as to his learning. Finally, he adjourned the business for a month to the 12th October, and entered into a correspondence with the Secretary of State, Sir Charles Hedges, who replied, after giving his own opinion:—

"I shall add no more, but that I have obeyed your commands in making such a representation of your scruples to her Majesty as you desire; and all I have in answer is that her Majesty expects that there should be no further delay in giving institution to Dr. Atterbury."

This order was complied with, and Dr. Atterbury regularly instituted on the 2nd of October, but the controversy raged for some time afterwards, though we need not follow it to the dregs. Atterbury complains that the bishop put several affronts on him, while keeping him in suspense, but he admits that he had tried to prevent the University of Oxford from granting Nicolson a doctor's degree. In point of temper there was probably little to choose between these two able and strong men.

Dr. Atterbury soon obtained a dispensation from the Queen exempting him from residence, but Dr. Todd, whom we have already mentioned as having been engaged in bitter controversy with Nicolson, was "only too ready to act jackal to the lion." The literary quarrel between Nicolson and Todd was much inflamed by a further quarrel over the appointment by Todd, who was vicar of Penrith, of one of his curates to be churchwarden of that parish. The bishop objected, and took steps to enforce his objections by declining to admit the curate to priest's orders, while Todd published "A Letter to a Person of Quality," in which he handled his diocesan with severity and freedom. Occasion was soon found for a quarrel between Atterbury and his chapter. Two minor canons having "misbehaved themselves in the vestry by kicking, boxing, and by words abusing" one another, were suspended and made to apologise in November, 1704; and in the following April, in the absence of the dean and Dr. Todd, they were restored to office. The dean and Dr. Todd promptly protested against this act as an infringement of the rights of the dean; the dean protesting "particularly on ye account of the right conferred on me, as dean, by the foundation charter of our church (lately retrieved and registered) to take cognisance of and punish all such offences and disorders." The dean, supported by Dr. Todd, ignored various acts of the vice-dean and chapter; he withheld his key of the chapter seal, when it was required in such cases as the renewal of leases or the presentation to livings, unless he had previously given his formal consent, by himself or his proxy.

This chapter was thus divided into the dean and Dr. Todd, who denied the validity of the statutes given by Henry VIII. to the dean and chapter, and the vice-dean and two canons, who upheld them. Matters soon came to a deadlock, and the vice-dean and his party appealed to the bishop to hold a visitation under the statutes. The bishop at first tried to arrange for some compromise. He was soon convinced of the uselessness of this, and determined to visit the cathedral. He issued his monition in August, 1707. Dean Atterbury at once questioned the right of the bishop to visit under the authority of "(pretended) local statutes." He and Dr. Todd refused to take any part in the proceedings. The visitation was, however, held in September, and the bishop's injunctions issued, ordering the statutes to be observed, and upholding the authority of the vice-dean and chapter. The proceedings were soon afterwards carried to the Queen's Bench, and the bishop excommunicated Dr. Todd, from which sentence the Court of Common Pleas relieved him by a prohibition direct to the bishop. This controversy had caused considerable excitement, the authority of the statutes of all the cathedrals of the new foundation being impugned. The matter passed out of the realms of law, and was quieted, so far as public interests were concerned, by the passing of the 6 Anne, 21, "An Act for the avoiding of Doubts and Questions touching the Statutes of divers Cathedral and Collegiate Churches." [1]

Nicolson found time while archdeacon and bishop to do a good deal of archæological and scientific

---

[1] The above is abbreviated from "The Statutes of the Cathedral Church of Carlisle," translated with an introduction by J. E. Prescott, D.D., 1879. Carlisle: C. Thurnams & Sons.

work, and from the original documents of his see he compiled some volumes of collections towards the history of the two counties, which form the basis on which Joseph Nicolson, his nephew, and Dr. Burn founded their " History of Westmorland and Cumberland." He also carried on a most voluminous correspondence with all the archæological scholars of his time.

To Nicolson the diocese owed one most pernicious legacy, the interference of ecclesiastical dignitaries in political contests, the source for about 130 or 140 years in Carlisle of quarrelling and ill-will, the memory of which has not yet died away. Thus, in the election for Carlisle, in 1710, the bishop's interference on behalf of the Whig candidate, Sir James Montague, was so marked as to bring upon his lordship the censure of the House of Commons, who summoned him to their bar. In an election petition that followed he was charged with threatening the cathedral choir with dismissal, if they did not vote for Montague.

In 1718, Bishop Nicolson was translated to Londonderry, and was much chagrined at finding he would have to reside in Ireland. On February 9, 1736-7, he was translated to the archbishopric of Cashel, but died suddenly on the 14th of that month.

Nicolson's successor at Carlisle, in 1718, was Samuel Bradford, a prebendary of Westminster, who found his way down to his see about a year after he had been appointed, and spent a fortnight in making a visitation of it. He was translated to Rochester in 1723, and was succeeded by John Waugh, a native of

Appleby, who held the see until 1734. To him succeeded Sir George Fleming, who died in 1747, aged eighty. Osbaldiston succeeded him, and held the see until he was translated to London in 1762. Then came Charles Lyttleton, who held the see for six years. During these episcopates the chief moving spirit in the diocese was Chancellor John Waugh, son of the bishop of that name. He was a staunch Whig. and he laboured assiduously to promote the Whig interests in Carlisle and Cumberland. During the outbreak of 1745 he arranged and managed an intelligence department for the English Government, and he organised a corps of guides for the Duke of Cumberland. He was rewarded with the deanery of Worcester, but continued to reside at Carlisle. He drafted the searching set of visitation queries put to the clergy at Bishop Osbaldistone's primary visitation in 1747. The terriers delivered in at this visitation contain most valuable information as to the diocese. This we are able to supplement by Chancellor Waugh's annotated copy of Bishop Nicolson's Miscellany Notes. From these it is obvious that since Nicolson's days considerable improvement had taken place throughout the diocese in respect both of the fabrics and furniture of the churches; the livings had been augmented, misappropriated endowments restored, and the number of discreditable parsons largely reduced. This seems mainly due to the administrative talents of Chancellor Waugh, who must have commanded the confidence of his bishops; he was helped as to augmentation of the livings by Dr. Bolton, dean of Carlisle, and by pecuniary assistance from Lady

Gower. Bishop Law next held the see of Carlisle, from 1768 to 1787, in conjunction with one of the golden stalls of Durham. It is recorded of him as a great merit that during his nineteen years' tenure of the see, he generally spent the summer months at Rose, a period of residence which would hardly satisfy the requirements of this century. He placed two of his sons in stalls in his cathedral, both of whom became bishops. Bishop Douglas, a distinguished scholar, next held the see for four years from 1787 to 1791. Then came Vernon, the first of a series of bishops of Carlisle, Vernon [Vernon Harcourt], Goodenough, Percy, Montagu Villiers, Waldegrave, and Goodwin, who lived at Rose Castle, made it their home, bound up with their dearest family interests, and did not reckon it a mere summer residence. Vernon had ten children born to him at Rose Castle, where he lived in a charming simplicity, which contrasted much with the subsequent splendour he kept at Bishopthorpe.

Bishops living in the diocese with and among their clergy have done much to elevate it from what it was when Nicolson made his famous notes, or even from the improved condition recorded of it in 1747 by Chancellor Waugh. Among the difficulties the bishops have had to contend with are, of course, the inadequacy of the stipends and the largeness of some of the parishes, many of which, in addition to the mother church, contained several chapelries : the sole endowment of these chapelries was a few shillings, which the inhabitants had at some remote period agreed to charge upon their estates. In consequence of their poverty these chapelries were served by unordained persons, called "readers," but in the time of George II. the bishops (Carlisle and Chester) came to a resolution that no one should officiate who was not in deacon's orders. The existing readers (one of whom is described as clogger, tailor, and butter-print-maker) were ordained without examination. This no way helped the incomes, and the reverend gentlemen eked out their stipends in various ways, assisted by contributions from their neighbours. In "The Old Church Clock," by the late Canon Parkinson, will be found an interesting account of the Rev. Robert Walker, curate of Seathwaite from 1736 to 1802, better known as "Wonderful Walker," which shows the poverty of the north-country livings, and the thrift and the piety of some of their incumbents, among whom were many scholars of high attainments, buried alive in remote mountain valleys. It must not be supposed that they were all like "Wonderful Walker"; on the contrary, there were too many no better in any way than the rude peasants among whom they lived, and of whom local legends preserve many quaint but disreputable stories. These, however, are now things of the past. But in the eighteenth century there were other abuses in the diocese of Carlisle. Pluralities abounded. Bishop Nicolson, in 1703, found Mr. Culcheth endeavouring to hold the livings of Stapleton, Upper Denton, and Farlam *in commendam* with that of Brampton, which last the Bishop computes at about £60 per annum. Stapleton he computes at about £20. Farlam, as late as 1750, was only £5. 15s.; and at that date Over Denton was only twenty shillings a year, so that this pluralist Culcheth enjoyed the magnificent income of something less than £90 a year, and yet he was comparatively a well-to-do man; for Chancellor Waugh, in 1747, seems to consider the perpetual curate of St. Mary's church, Carlisle, well provided for with an annual income of £50. But if Culcheth was well off, his four sets of parishioners were not. The bishop describes the church at Brampton as—

"in a slovenly pickle: dark, black, and ill seated. The Quire is yet more nasty."

Of Stapleton he records,—

"The Quire here is most intolerably Scandaleous: No Glass in the Windows: no Ascent to anything like an altar; no Flooring; no seats . . . . The parishioners follow the example of their Parson, and have the Body of the Church in as nasty a pickle as the Quire. The roof so miserably shattered that it cannot be safe sitting under it . . . . onely some few scraps of a common-prayer-book, and an insufferably torn Bible of the old Translation. There was no Surplice to be found: nor did ever any such thing (as far as any present could remember) belong to this Church. One of 'em told us that sometimes on Easter-day, the Parson has brought a surplice with him: had Administer'd ye Sacrament in it: But even that Ordinance (amongst the rest) was most commonly celebrated without one."

We may add that the dead at Stapleton were buried without any service, and that the road between Brampton and Stapleton was impassable in winter. Farlam was more decent than the bishop expected; there was a curate there, who seemed to pick up a poor and precarious salary by keeping a school in the

Quire. Over or Upper Denton the bishop did not visit. This was the state of things in 1704.

Let us refer to Chancellor Waugh's notes and see if there was any improvement by the year 1747. Brampton certainly was better off; the income was improved,—£90 annually,—and the service held, except on the first Sunday in the month, in a decent chapel made in the hospital in the town. On the first Sunday it was held in the parish church, which is at some distance. A new vicar was just appointed, who complained that the late vicar had left the vicarage in a bad state, but the chancellor says his son was answerable for it and able to pay. Brampton was clearly improved. Stapleton, in 1747, had a vicar of its own, who was instituted in 1714, and the chancellor says :—

"Stapleton . . . . I never saw the place, but from the Indecency of the Man (the vicar) and accounts I have had of it, all in very poor order."

But Farlam and Over Denton were, in 1747, held together with the neighbouring parish of Lanercost; not one of these parishes possessed a residence for the vicar; from Farlam and Denton he drew the magnificent incomes, already mentioned, of £5. 15s. and of 20s.; while Lanercost was worth, on the average, about £20, painfully made up by the collection of the following dues over a parish which covered 40,000 acres of land :—

"For a cow and calf	3d.
,, a quey and calf	2d.
,, a farrow cow	1d.
,, a foal	4d.

For a winter stand of bees	4d.
,, a cast	2d.
,, every communicant	3d.
,, every family for holy bread	2d.
,, plough penny	1d.
,, customary pennies by such families as keep no plough	3d.

Lanercost, Farlam, and Denton had been, before the Reformation, appropriate to the priory of Lanercost, and served by inmates of that house. After the Reformation, when the property of the priory had been granted to lay hands by the Crown, the Crown grantees grasped all that they could, and left as little as possible for the parish. By means of Queen Anne's Bounty, and in other ways, those three livings were gradually augmented; but they were held together until within this century, the united income being barely £100 per annum, while the highly respected incumbent could not possibly fulfil the duties of the three parishes under his charge, though he did what he could. At the present time Farlam has an income of £160 per annum and a vicarage house, while the church was rebuilt in 1859. Its population is 1585 persons. Lanercost is now worth £300 a year, which includes £80 from the trustees of the Earl of Carlisle, while its church (in the nave of Lanercost Abbey) and its vicarage are among the most charming in the diocese. Its population is 11,000. Over Denton, in 1808, was augmented to £46. 5s. per annum. It was held with Lanercost until 1858, whose vicar occasionally went over on Sunday afternoons and held a service, if a congregation appeared. Over Denton is now merged in

Gilsland, and has two churches and a vicarage-house with an income of £171 per annum, and a population of 330 persons.

From this account we may see that the bishops of Carlisle in the eighteenth century were frequently in a dilemma: if they allowed pluralities, the parishes were neglected; if they disallowed them, the parsons could not live. Thus, in 1737, Bishop Fleming severed the parishes of Dearham and Gilcrux, which had for long been held together on account of their poverty. In 1747 Chancellor Waugh complains "that neither of them were left a tolerable substance for the incumbent," Gilcrux being about £15 per annum, and Dearham probably the same. The vicarages were mere thatched cottages.

Chancellor Waugh's notion of a sufficient income for a vicar was not extravagant; he records, apparently with satisfaction, that St. Cuthbert's and St. Mary's churches in Carlisle were, in 1747, held by perpetual curates, who were also minor canons of the cathedral, and who each enjoyed an income, as curate and minor canon, of £50 per annum, without house or residence. One of these two curates, the Rev. George Braithwaite, the vicar of St. Mary's, was, in 1747, supposed to be 104 years of age, and was blind; he had held his two valuable pieces of preferment, curacy and minor canonry, for sixty-eight years, and had previously been singing boy and singing man in the cathedral, having commenced as singing boy at the Restoration; in 1747 he was still officiating at baptisms, marriages, and funerals, but his brother minor canons took the Sunday service for him.

To leave this digression, and to return to the clerical incomes of the eighteenth century, it is clear that in 1747 £50 was considered by Chancellor Waugh a sufficient income for an incumbent; between £50 and £100 a good income; and anything over that wealth. The chancellor's own living of Caldbeck he reckons at £150 a year clear, and he also held Stanwix, which was £90, in addition to his canonry and chancellorship. Greystoke was £300 a year, and was held by Archdeacon (afterwards bishop) Law, together with Great Salkeld, which was worth £70 *per annum*. The living of Arthuret Chancellor Waugh values at £170 per annum; Crosthwaite (Keswick) at £120; Penrith at about £85, or more, out of which a curate must be kept; Kirkbythore at £140, after paying £20 each to the chapelries of Sowerby and Milburn; and Appleby, £120.

We have already mentioned the chapelries as possessed of very small endowments. Here is a list of chapelries in the barony of Kendal, as cited by Canon Ware from Burn and Nicolson's "County History":—

Old Hutton with Holmscales, £6. 13s. 4d.; Grayrigg, £6. 13s. 4d.; Selside, £3. 19s.; Burneside, £6. 13s. 4d.; Longsleddale, £5. 2s. 10d.; Kentmere, £6; Staveley, £6. 13s. 4d.; Ings, £2. 16s. 8d.; Crook, £3. 16s. 6d.; Winster, £3. 19s.; Underbarrow, £6. 4s. 2d.; Langdale, £6. 4s. 3d.; Troutbeck, £4. 12s. 3d.; Crosthwaite and Lyth,

£5. 8s. 10d. ; Witherslack, £6. 13s. 4d. ; Preston Patrick, £3. 6s. 8d. ; Furthbank, £3 ; Ambleside, £14 originally, but reduced to £12. 4s. 11d."[1]

The date of origin of these chapelries is difficult to ascertain ; some were consecrated in the sixteenth century, but had apparently been licensed at a much earlier period for prayer and preaching. The reason of their origin is clear ; the inhabitants of outlying and remote districts in enormous parishes like those of Greystoke, Crosthwaite, St. Bees, Kendal, Kirkby Stephen, Kirkby Lonsdale, &c., found it inconvenient or impossible to attend the Mother Church, and so petitioned the bishop, with consent of the incumbent of the Mother Church, for licence to have a chapel ; the bishop, before granting his licence, would require an endowment, which at one time was to be not less than six marks, afterwards raised to twelve. This the petitioners bound themselves to provide, and by deed charged upon their lands, sometimes in proportion to the rent they paid the lord of the manor, sometimes at so much a seat in the chapel. But they still looked to the parish church as their Mother Church, and on the greater festivals trooped there in a body for the Sacrament, headed by their curate and their banner ; thither, too, they resorted for burial. Gradually the bishops consecrated the chapelries, the sacraments were administered in them, and the dead buried beside them. The curates of the chapelries

[1] See papers on *Killington*, *Kirkby Lonsdale*, by Canons Ware and Simpson. "Transactions Cumberland and Westmorland Antiquarian and Archæological Society," vol. viii., pp. 93 and 109.

augmented their salaries by teaching school, generally in the chapels. To get a school and schoolmaster was as much the object of the subscribers to these chapel salaries as to get a chapel and curate. The subscribers frequently in turn provided the curate with a "whittle-gate,"[1]—that is, his board,—or "the run of his teeth." Thus, prior to the Reformation, sufficient provision was made for the maintenance of a celibate curate, often sent from some monastic house, if there was one, as at St. Bees, interested in the Mother Church. But after the Reformation, with the introduction of a married clergy, and the fall in the purchasing power of money, the salaries became insufficient, and the unordained readers we have already spoken of were all that could be obtained.

The origin of these chapelries requires to be made known; their salaries are charges on the land, but the deeds creating the charges are at this date rarely forthcoming, and in some places the landowners, who are liable to them, are beginning to repudiate the payment on the ground that they are voluntary payments, were abolished with church-rates, or other frivolous and shabby pretence.

In connexion with these chapelries and the smaller livings in the diocese of Carlisle (as extended in 1856), it may not be inappropriate to mention the extraordinary length of time during which some in-

[1] The rector of St. Ninian's church at Brougham, in Westmorland, still has right of "whittle-gate" on Sundays at Hornby Hall, if he pleases to claim it.

cumbents held office. The Rev. George Braithwaite and the Rev. Robert Walker (Wonderful Walker) have already been mentioned. The first was admitted minor canon of Carlisle cathedral on June 25, 1679, and appointed perpetual curate of St. Mary's church, Carlisle, about the same time. These valuable pieces of preferment he retained until his death in 1753, at the supposed age of 110, and a tenure of office of 74 years. His age may possibly be exaggerated, and he may not have been a centenarian, but there can be no doubt about the 74 years if Chancellor Waugh's extract from the chapter-books of the date of his admission is correct. Wonderful Walker died in 1802 in the 93rd year of his age and the 67th of his curacy at Seathwaite, which, when Walker first accepted it, was worth £5 per annum. In the middle of the century Walker valued it at £17. 10s. per annum. His successor, the Rev. Edward Tyson, held the curacy from 1802 to 1854, having previously been Walker's curate for seven years. Two incumbents thus held Seathwaite for 118 years. The chapelry of Threlkeld, near Keswick, had only three incumbents in 153 years,—namely, Alexander Naughley, 1705 to 1756; Thomas Edmondson, 1756 to 1798; and Thomas Collinson, 1798 to 1858. A melancholy and curious account of the first of these incumbents,—a man of extraordinary attainments in literature,—who eked out a scanty stipend by teaching the classics and mathematics, is given in Hutchinson's "History of Cumberland," vol. i., p. 422. He clearly went mad. His successor, Edmondson, was an exemplary and worthy man. Threlkeld is not unique. In another fellside parish three incumbencies covered a similar period, and each incumbent reigned for about half a century. One committed suicide, and one, if not both the others were deprived for drinking. The terrible isolation from all educated society told at last. These cases are sad contrasts to the bright picture of cheerful and Christian piety presented of Wonderful Walker in "The Old Church Clock." Parallels to him in piety and poverty can be instanced:—the Rev. Josiah Relph, the poet priest of Sebergham, where he supplemented a stipend of £25 per annum by teaching school, occupies a high place in the list of Cumberland worthies of the last century.[1] Another Cumberland poet and scholar succeeded Relph at Sebergham, though not immediately, the Rev. Thomas Denton.

At the beginning of the eighteenth century many of the poorer livings (if the name is appropriate) were held by Scotch Episcopalians, who had been driven out of preferments in their own country. Threlkeld was held from 1698 to 1705 by Andrew Naughley, father of the unhappy Alexander; Andrew was an Episcopalian clergyman of reputation at Stow, in the Lothians, but refusing from conscientious motives to sign the covenant, and siding with the Marquis of Montrose, he was deposed and banished. He and

---

[1] Whelan, in his "History of Cumberland," states that Relph died "from actual want of the necessaries of life"; that is not so, for his will, proved at Carlisle in 1743, shows he died worth £227.

his wife trudged on foot, with a pony carrying their children in panniers, to Threlkeld, and he accepted the vacant cure there. He was a scholar, and educated his son Alexander, and out of his stipend of £12 per annum managed to send him to the University of Edinburgh. Another ejected Episcopalian, Kinneir, once rector of Annan, in Scotland, was curate of Sebergham from 1699 to 1735. He was a man of worth and piety, and was followed to Sebergham by some of his flock, who settled in the parish. At Bewcastle, the curate, Mr. Allen, is mentioned by Bishop Nicolson, as "a poor, ejected Episcopalian of the Scottish nation." There were one or two more with poor preferment in the diocese, all men of good character; and others found employment as schoolmasters, a position from which many in the diocese of Carlisle rose to high preferment in the Church. Thus at Sebergham, Relph was followed as schoolmaster by Blain, Halifax, and Jackson, all three classical scholars of high attainments. The first kept school at Sebergham, in a mud hut, and was afterwards master of Wigton Grammar School, and domestic and examining chaplain to Bishop Law; the second succeeded Blain at Sebergham, and at Wigton Grammar School, and became incumbent of Westward; the third, mathematician as well as classic, became vicar of Morland, and was the intimate friend of Archdeacon Paley.

Chancellor Waugh, at various times from 1730 to 1747, collected statistics as to the number of families of Dissenters in the diocese. As these are utilised in the foot-notes to each parish in Hutchinson's

"Cumberland," a few parishes need only be given here:—

	No. of families.	Presbyterians.	Quakers.	Papists.	Anabaptists.
S. Mary's, Carlisle, 1747 ...	177	14	7	0	0
S. Cuthbert's, Carlisle, 1747	291	9	10	0	0
Warwick, 1747	47	0	4	3	0
Greystoke, 1747	347	16	15	1	0
Brampton, 1730	236	52	1	2	0
Arthuret, 1730	294	2	3	1	0
Crosthwaite, 1730	550	20	4	0	0
Kirkby Stephen, 1747	607	4	4	3	1
Appleby, 1730	160	0	0	0	0
Wigton, 1730	475	—	63	—	—
Holm Cultram	479	4	30	0	4

SEAL OF CORPORATION OF CARLISLE.

CHAPTER XI.

THE NINETEENTH CENTURY.

A GLANCE through the pages of the Carlisle Diocesan Calendar shows that almost the whole of the machinery by which the diocese is worked has been recast, or invented since the beginning of the present century. Under, therefore, the title of the "Nineteenth Century," it is now proposed to give some account of such machinery, including under the term the educational and charitable institutions connected in their origin with the Church of England.

It is not necessary to repeat here, what has already been stated in the first chapter of this little book, as to the enlargement of the diocese in 1856 by the addition of a new archdeaconry to the solitary one which, from Bishop Æthelwulf's consecration to Bishop Percy's death, constituted the diocese of Carlisle; and as to the more recent rearrangement and division of those two archdeaconries into three. Nor is it necessary to here repeat the information there given as to the deaneries and the parishes.

When the nineteenth century opened, Vernon-Harcourt was Bishop of Carlisle. In 1808 he became Archbishop of York, and was succeeded at Carlisle by Dr. Goodenough, Dean of Rochester, and eminent as a botanist. A magnificent herbarium formed by him in the last century was, on his death, given to the Carlisle Museum, where it long remained useless and neglected, until the corporation of Carlisle wisely transferred it to the authorities at the Kew Botanical Gardens. Traditions still linger in Carlisle of the stately presence and commanding figure of Dr. Goodenough, as he appeared for the first time in his cathedral,[1] and of the Spartan discipline he maintained among his numerous progeny. Three of his sons held stalls in Carlisle cathedral, while his daughters were provided for by snug little arrangements out of the salaries of the officials of the Consistory Court of Carlisle. The Goodenoughs in the cathedral stalls of Carlisle were most energetic in carrying on the evil policy of interfering unduly in the political contests at Carlisle, and figure frequently in the local political caricatures and skits, as also did the more celebrated dean, Dr. Isaac Milner, president of Queen's College, Cambridge. Milner held the deanery from 1792 to 1820, thus almost covering the episcopates of Vernon-Harcourt and of Goodenough, 1791 to 1827. With both these prelates he was on friendly terms, though belonging to a widely different school of religious thought to what they did. This appears from a remark made by Dr. Paley to a friend:—

"Why, yes; I told the Bishop of Carlisle [Dr. Vernon-Harcourt] that about the evangelical doctrines themselves I must leave him to judge, but that if he chose to hear them urged with

---

[1] It should be recorded that he was the last Bishop of Carlisle to wear a wig, and Milner the last dean.

great ability and placed in the most striking point of view, he must go and hear our dean."[1]

Paley in a letter writes:—

"When the Dean of Carlyle preaches you may walk upon the heads of the people. All the meetings [*i.e.*, the Dissenters], attend to hear him. He is, indeed, a powerful preacher."

Of the congregations the dean had to preach to, a graphic picture is presented in a letter from the dean's brother, the Reverend Joseph Milner, vicar of Hull, to a friend:—

"The people here [Carlisle], the aborigines, are a well-behaved, simple people; the refinement, shall I say, or the lewdness and impudence of the southern part of our island, they know not. They have the sample, I take it, of the manners of the whole country in the time of James I.; but they are withal very ignorant in religion: they wander as sheep without a shepherd. They seem, however, open to conviction; they have conscience. There are, here, some Methodist and Dissenting interests, but feeble and of little weight, nor is there a Dissenter here of any popularity, or, as it should seem, of any religious zeal.[2] What a fine field for a pastor steady, fervent, intelligent, and chari-

---

[1] "The Life of Isaac Milner," by his niece, p. 116.

[2] The Dissenting interest in Carlisle in 1797, the date of this letter, consisted of a Presbyterian chapel in Fisher-street, with a regular succession of ministers from 1688; a chapel in Annetwell-street, built for a Presbyterian congregation about 1780, then in the hands of Lady Glenorchy's connexion; a Friends' Meeting-house in Fisher-street, belonging to a Friends' Meeting in Carlisle, founded by George Fox; a Wesleyan Methodist chapel, also in Fisher-street, built in 1786. It may be mentioned that from the Reformation to 1799 there was no place of Roman Catholic worship in Carlisle. The celebrated Dr. Robert Henry was minister of the Presbyterian chapel from 1748 to 1760.

table! Pray ye to the Lord of the harvest, &c. I inculcate this duty on those I have access to; for it is a pitiable thing to see the ignorance of this place,—ignorance, rather than contempt of Divine truth, is its character. The Lord may, in His time, send them a supply. At present their state is lamentable beyond expression." [1]

This letter was written in 1797, and in it Joseph Milner makes one exception to his universal condemnation:—

"Old Mr. Fawcett . . . . who, I am glad to find in his old age, seems to be sitting at the feet of Jesus, and hearing his word."

In the year 1800 a son of "old Mr. Fawcett" was appointed,—greatly through the influence of Dean Milner,—perpetual curate of St. Cuthbert's church, Carlisle,—a post he retained until his death in 1851, at the age of eighty-two. In the Rev. John Fawcett, perpetual curate of St. Cuthbert's, the "aborigines" of Carlisle found a pastor such as Joseph Milner considered they required, "steady, fervent, intelligent, and charitable." Mr. Fawcett became, in succession to Dean Milner, the leader of the Evangelical party in Carlisle; and, though he had his enemies and his detractors, he attained a position of greater popularity and power in Carlisle than any clergyman had ever done before or has since, although nigh forty years have by now passed over his grave, and although changes have been effected in Carlisle churches, and notably in his own church, which he would have denounced with vigour, yet his influence is by no means dead. Those who recollect him, his

[1] "The Life of Isaac Milner," p. 130.

venerable appearance, and his preaching, will appreciate Dean Milner's remark about him, "That man is rich in the Scriptures."

In 1812 Bishop Goodenough started a project for establishing in Carlisle a school on the system known as Dr. Bell's, or the National system. A strong difference of opinion arose between the bishop and the dean over the religious difficulty; the bishop insisted that the children should be instructed in the liturgy and catechism of the Church of England, and should go with their teachers regularly to church every Sunday. To this last the dean and an influential party strongly objected, but the bishop carried his point,[1] and the school, long known in Carlisle as the Central School, was founded.[2] To this school Dr. Goodenough paid the most assiduous attention; giving it his personal superintendence, and spending in it several hours daily; nor did the controversy between bishop and dean in any way interfere with their friendship, or prevent the dean from supporting a proposal that the chapter should subscribe to the school. Another difference (again a friendly one) arose between bishop and dean on the occasion of the establishment in Carlisle, by the dean in 1813, of an Auxiliary Bible Society. There existed all over the country great differences of opinion on the propriety of Churchmen associating with Dissenters in the management of Bible So

---

[1] See "Life of Isaac Milner," chap. xxiv., for the correspondence between the bishop and dean.
[2] *Ibid.*

cieties,[1] and the bishop stood aloof from the Carlisle Society, whose presidency was accepted by the then Lord Morpeth (George, sixth Earl of Carlisle). Of this society Mr. Fawcett was a great advocate, as also of the Church Missionary Society, of which a branch was formed in Carlisle in 1817. Of it the dean accepted the presidency, but he stood alone so far as regarded the cathedral clergy; the bishop also remained aloof, and among the laity few persons of rank or station enrolled their names in the list of supporters. A society for the relief of necessitous widows and orphans of the clergy in the diocese of Carlisle was founded in 1819, with apparently the concurrence of all the local church parties. This society only covers the ancient diocese, but the portion added in 1856 is covered by the Kendal Clerical Charity, which dates from 1786. In 1814 a local branch of the Society for Promoting Christian Knowledge was in existence in Carlisle, of which the Rev. John Brown was secretary and treasurer. A branch of the Society for Propagating the Gospel was established in 1835. Most of the other great Church societies have at various times established branches in the diocese, but so long as the Fawcett influence was in full vigour, and during the episcopates of Bishops Villiers and Waldegrave, the societies popular with the Evangelical party received the most support in and near the city of Carlisle. Of late years the tendency has been much more to equality.

Coming to purely local societies connected with

[1] Much information on this subject is in "The Life of Isaac Milner," chaps. xxiii., xxiv., and xxv.

the ancient diocese of Carlisle, in addition to the Society for the Relief of Necessitous Widows and Orphans, founded by Bishop Goodenough in 1819, a Carlisle Diocesan Clergy-Aid Society was established by Bishop Percy in 1838, the object of the Society being to aid in supplying assistant curates to aged or disabled incumbents of inadequate income, and to poorly-endowed parishes, which, from their area or population, require the services of two or more clergymen. The Carlisle Diocesan Education Society was founded in 1855, by Bishop Percy and Dean Tait (Archbishop of Canterbury), and others for the promotion and improvement of education throughout the diocese. During the earlier years of its existence the work of the Society was of a general character and considerable sums were spent on school building, extension, books, and apparatus. On the passing of the Elementary Education Act of 1870, the Society reconsidered its position, and came to the conclusion that the objects for which it was instituted would be best carried out by taking in hand as its special duty the important work of inspection and examination in religious knowledge, which the law of the land now left to voluntary agencies. A diocesan inspector of religious education was, therefore, appointed by the Society in 1872, and an assistant inspector has since been added. In the year just past the religious examination of 31,884 children has been inspected and reported upon, and 2,636 children and 150 pupil teachers have been examined on paper. Thirty-nine Board Schools have also been examined by the diocesan inspector. The Carlisle Diocesan Church

Extension Society was established in 1862 by Bishop Waldegrave with the fourfold object (i.) of promoting the increase of church accommodation within the diocese, by aiding in the erection of new churches, and in the restoration and enlargement of old ones ; (ii.) of aiding in the erection, or purchase, or enlargement of parsonages ; (iii.) of assisting in augmenting benefices of small income ; and (iv.) of promoting the provision of mission-rooms. Since its inauguration in 1862, up to the end of 1888, the Society has dispensed in grants £57,163. 6s. 4d., which sum has been met from public and private sources by the sum of £316,974. 10s. 10d. The result has been the building or restoring 128 churches, the building or improving of 94 parsonages, and the building or maintaining of 16 mission-rooms. The work done by this Society in the diocese cannot be too highly estimated.

The diocese also has a Clerical Training Fund established in 1873, and a Missionary Students' Fund established in 1874. both doing good work. There is also a Church of England Temperance Society, of which the bishop is president. The Diocesan Clergy Aid Society (already spoken of) has the administration of two very useful funds. One, the Boutflower Memorial Fund for sick clergymen of the diocese, established in memory of the late Archdeacon Boutflower, who died in 1883 : grants from it are available to enable a sick clergyman to obtain professional or other aid, rest from work, or change of air. The other, the Harvey Goodwin Rest Fund, which has been recently established by a few friends of Bishop Goodwin, in commemoration of his seventieth birthday; its purpose is to enable clergymen of small means to obtain a holiday from home, even though not suffering from sickness. These societies cover the whole diocese, but in addition to them there are many local ones, some of which, like the Carlisle Female Visiting Society, date from the last century.

Dr. Goodwin, on his appointment to the diocese of Carlisle, lost no time in establishing a Diocesan Conference. This has proved a most valuable wheel in the diocesan machinery, and has succeeded in eliciting weighty expressions of opinion from both clergy and laity on various important questions that have from time to time arisen, locally and nationally. The constitution of the Conference is as follows:—

CARLISLE DIOCESAN CONFERENCE.[1]
CONSTITUTION AS REVISED, 1886.

1. A Conference, consisting partly of Clergymen and partly of Laymen, shall be from time to time convened under the presidency of the Bishop of the Diocese, for the purpose of taking counsel concerning questions affecting the religious and social interests of the country, and specially concerning those which immediately affect the well-being and efficiency of the Church of England.
2. The following Clergymen shall be members of the Conference:—The Dean and the Canons Residentiary, the Archdeacons, the Honorary Canons resident in the Diocese, the Rural Deans, the Proctors for the Clergy in Convocation,

---

[1] A regard to space compels us to abbreviate by the omission of some details. The revision in 1886 mainly consisted in eliminating a large *ex officio* lay element, whose members did not attend.

the Diocesan Inspector of Schools, and four Clergy elected from each Rural Deanery by the Ruridecanal Chapter.

3. The following Laymen (being Members of the Church of England) shall be Members of the Conference :—The Chancellor of the Diocese; a number not exceeding twelve, invited each year by the Bishop; and a number not exceeding eight, nominated for each Rural Deanery by the Lay Members of the Ruridecanal Meeting.

4. The Standing Committee shall have power to add to the Conference a number of Members not exceeding four, who may be either Clergymen or Laymen.

The Hon. Treasurer and the Hon. Secretaries shall be *ex officio* Members.

5. Any elected Member, Clerical or Lay, failing to attend the Meetings of the Conference for two consecutive years shall cease to be a Member, but may be re-elected : and it shall be the duty of the Ruridecanal Chapter or Meeting to fill up his place for the remainder of the period for which he was elected.

RULES FOR THE CONDUCT OF THE CONFERENCE.

1. The Bishop shall be Chairman.

2. The subjects discussed shall be such as shall be appointed by the Bishop, or as shall be introduced by permission of the Conference, due notice being given of any subject which any Member wishes to introduce.

Any resolution intended to be moved by any Member reading a paper, or introducing a subject, shall be forwarded to one of the Secretaries for the purpose of being printed and placed in the hands of the Members before the Session at which such resolution is to be moved.

3. In cases of voting upon any question, the Members of the Conference, Clerical or Lay, shall vote in general as one body. It shall, however, be competent to any five Members of the Conference to demand that the votes of Clerical and Lay Members be taken separately : in which case a resolution shall not be regarded as carried, unless it be carried by a majority in each body, the Bishop in all cases having a casting vote.

4. As a general rule, Members of the Conference shall only speak once upon each question, and for a limited time; fifteen minutes being allowed to the first speaker, and ten minutes to subsequent speakers.

5. The representatives of the press shall be admitted.

6. A Standing Committee shall be appointed annually, whose office it shall be to confer with the Bishop of the Diocese on matters connected with the Conference, and to transact any necessary business when the Conference is not in session: and the said Committee shall consist of the Secretaries, the Treasurer, and twelve other Members to be named by the Conference, and of whom six shall be Clergymen and six Laymen.

THE RURAL DEANERY.

1. The Ruridecanal *Chapter* shall be constituted as follows:—
   A. The Rural Dean (chairman).
   B. All Incumbents in the Deanery.
   C. All Priests officiating in the Deanery with the Bishop's Licence.
   D. All Clergymen resident in the Deanery, who may receive an invitation from the official members of the Chapter (A, B, C).

The Archdeacon shall have the right of attending any Chapter within his Archdeaconry, but shall not have the right of taking the chair.

A book containing the minutes of the Chapter shall be kept by the Rural Dean.

The subjects discussed at the Chapter shall be (1) such as may be directed by the Bishop; (2) such as may be agreed upon by the Members of the Chapter.

The number of meetings to be held in the year, and all other details of arrangement, must be settled by each Rural Deanery for itself.

2. The Ruridecanal *Meeting* shall be constituted as follows:—
   E. The Members of the Chapter as already set forth.
   F. Two Lay Representatives (being members of the Church of England) to be elected yearly by the Laity of each Parish, District, or Church within the Deanery, at a Vestry to be called by the In-

cumbent for that purpose, notice of the Meeting to be given, if the Incumbent thinks fit, in Church on the Sunday previous, and a written or printed notice to be affixed to the Church door. The election may take place in the Easter vestry meeting, at the discretion of the Incumbent. The names of the persons elected to be sent by the Incumbent to the Rural Dean.

G. The Lay Representatives from the Deanery to the Diocesan Conference.

The Members representing the Deanery at the last Conference shall be considered to be in office until the conclusion of the Meeting called for the election of their successor.

H. Masters of Church of England Elementary Schools, in such proportions as each Ruridecanal Meeting may decide.

The Ruridecanal Meeting may, if it please, invite certain other Laymen (being Members of the Church of England) not exceeding in number one-third of the Churches within the Deanery.

The practical arrangements for the *Meetings* shall be strictly analogous to those for the *Chapters*.

Reports of Ruridecanal discussions must be sent to the President at least one month before the date fixed for the Meeting of the Conference, in order to ensure the insertion of them in the general report of the results of the Chapters and Meetings laid before the Conference.

In the first six years under the original constitution the average attendance was 57 clergy and 51 laymen, a total of 920. In the next nine years the average attendance was 59 clergy and 51 laymen, total 110. In 1887, the first year after the amended constitution, the attendance out of a total of 267 members, was 141,—namely, 82 clergy and 59 laymen; in 1888 the attendance, out of 265 members, was 142,—

namely, 89 out of 109 clergymen, and 53 out of 155 laymen. The annual printed reports of the proceedings of the Conference contain many papers and debates of the highest interest.

Since the establishment of the Diocesan Conference it has been held regularly every year, with one exception,—1884. In that year the Church Congress was held in Carlisle, under the presidency of the Bishop of Carlisle, who, in his address to the Diocesan Conference of the following year, spoke as follows:—

"Whatever may have been the fruits of the Congress [at Carlisle] for the Church at large, I have had abundant proof that advantages have accrued to this city and diocese for which I feel deeply thankful to the Dispenser of all Events. Increased respect for the National Church; increased apprehension of her influence, activity, and power; a drawing together of the hearts of those who love the things of God, though not seeing things ecclesiastical with the same eyes,—these are a few, and only a few, of the results which I venture to attribute to the Carlisle Church Congress."[1]

In addition to the Diocesan Conference at Carlisle, the rural deans of the diocese assemble annually for two days at Rose Castle to hold consultations, and conferences are frequently held there of experts in education, and other subjects of interest to the diocese.

The Church army has recently received the official

[1] Advantage was taken of the opening of this Congress to present the Bishop of Carlisle with a very beautiful pastoral staff for the use of himself and his successors in the see. The presentation was made by Lord Muncaster on behalf of a large body of subscribers, clerical and lay.

sanction of the Bishop of Carlisle, and has been introduced into parishes in Carlisle and Workington with, it is believed, good effect.

Another wheel is shortly to be introduced into the diocesan machinery by the appointment of a suffragan bishop. The announcement by Dr. Goodwin of his intention to apply for a suffragan bishop somewhat startled the diocese, people fearing that untoward necessity had arisen. All, however, are rejoiced to hear that, after an episcopate of twenty years' duration, and after passing his seventieth birthday, the bishop recognises the necessity of curtailing his almost preternatural activity in travelling about his diocese, and of delegating some of his duties to another. Dr. Goodwin is too valuable to, and too valued in, his diocese for the inhabitants to contentedly watch him spend himself when he should spare himself. It is their fervent hope that the assistance now contemplated may ensure his long remaining with unimpaired powers in his present position.

Here, perhaps, is the place to mention a scheme which Dr. Goodwin promoted in 1877, with a view of circulating in each parish the financial history of the parish itself, and so encouraging the parishioners to look upon the parochial endowments as a property in which they have a permanent interest, the idea being that this would lead the parishioners to oppose confiscation even when proposed upon the fascinating plea of religious equality, and would also put the extinguisher upon many falsehoods. Dr. Goodwin invited each parochial clergyman to draw up a strict and clear account of the source of the endowments in each parish; and at a meeting of rural deans, held at Rose Castle, a small committee of experts was appointed to act as referees and advisers. In a certain number of parishes the work has already been done, and in others it is being done; but many difficulties hinder it from being generally carried out.

At the commencement of this chapter we alluded to the educational and charitable institutions of the diocese. It is not proposed here to go into the history of the hospitals, dispensaries, and other kindred institutions of the diocese; but they have one and all found their best friends among the bishops, the deans, and the dignitaries of the diocese. The Cumberland Infirmary almost owes its being to Dr. Percy, and it owes its enlargement to Drs. Goodwin and Close, and these three, the late Chancellor Burton, and the canons of Carlisle have supplied much of the administrative talent that has run the infirmary. The Convalescent Institution at Silloth, the Border Counties Home for Incurables, and other charities, will ever be connected with the name of Burton, and at the present day, when the committee of a charitable institution gets into a difficulty, financial or administrative, the cry is at once raised, "Let us go and consult the bishop," who never fails to suggest a way over, through, or round the trouble.

The diocese of Carlisle, as extended in 1556, has always been rich in educational foundations, endowed or not, which mostly had their origin in the sixteenth century, though they may have succeeded older schools, connected with dissolved religious houses. For accounts of these schools and of their endowments the curious must refer to the usual books and sources of information; a list of their founders and benefactors, royal, archiepiscopal,[1] episcopal, and otherwise, would show the close connexion originally intended to be established between these schools and the Church of England, a connexion now much modified, in some cases by the adoption of schemes under the Endowed Schools Acts, which transferred the management from purely ecclesiastical authorities to bodies composed of *ex officio* representatives and co-optative members. These schools have had, like all other schools, their ups and downs; but some of them have occupied very high positions indeed, and have turned out scholars who rose to the highest places in the Church, frequently to the episcopal bench. Such schools were Appleby, where bishops Smith and Waugh received their education, as also did Barlow, bishop of Lincoln; Lancelot Addison, dean of Lichfield; Mr. Secretary of State Robinson (Jack Robinson), Thomas Fothergill and Thomas Collinson, both provosts of Queen's College, Oxford; Sir Joseph Yates, Justice of the King's Bench, &c. Bampton, where Gibson, bishop of London, the learned editor of Camden; Oswald, bishop of Raphoe; Burton, dean of Kildare; Sir J. Wilson, Justice of the Pleas; and many more divines and scholars, emanated. One master of this school

[1] Archbishops Grindal and Sandys both founded schools in the diocese of which they were natives,—the one at St. Bees, the other at Hawkshead.

boasted that he had educated more than 300 priests. Heversham, responsible for Preston, bishop of Ferns and Killala; and Watson, bishop of Llandaff. Kendal, for Law, bishop of Carlisle. Kirkby Lonsdale, for John Bell, Q.C. Winton, for Chancellor Burn. Great Blencow, for Lord Chief Justice Ellenborough. Bromfield, for the Rev. Jonathan Bouchen. Carlisle, for Thomas, bishop of Rochester; Tullie, dean of Carlisle, and J. A. D. Carlyle, chancellor of Carlisle. There was never, throughout the sixteenth, seventeenth, and eighteenth centuries, lack of opportunity in the diocese of Carlisle for those who would work to obtain a sound education at very moderate cost, frequently gratuitously. But in the end of the eighteenth century, and more so in the nineteenth century, these schools fell largely into decay; one cause was, that the local gentry commenced to send their sons from home to be educated at the great public schools, or at academies, where they met only persons of their own rank; the other, that these schools did not move with the times; they frequently taught Latin and Greek, and Latin and Greek only; and when these languages were the only passport to distinction all classes were satisfied with them. But a demand arose for other knowledge, available in the commercial and engineering and other lines of life; and boys were sent away to other places to acquire such, and also to unlearn the local accent. Many of these schools have now awoke, and in one way or another have been regenerated: some of them seem to have bright futures before them.

The capstone to this educational edifice was the exclusive privileges which natives of Cumberland and Westmorland enjoyed at Queen's College, Oxford. Were the lists of matriculations at that college published and the careers of the students followed out, the number of priests of the Church of England that would be proved natives of the two counties would be as extraordinary as the heights in the Church to which many of them rose from being mere peasant lads. The vast majority of the natives of Cumberland and Westmorland who went to universities selected the Church as their profession, but many attained to high positions in political and legal life. Changes at Oxford have largely deprived the natives of the two counties of the preferences they enjoyed at Queen's College, Oxford; these changes have not been for the educational interests of the diocese.

But if the capstone of the edifice has been somewhat dislodged, new stepping-stones have been placed at the foot thereof by the establishment, in 1878, of "The George Moore Educational Trust," for promoting the improved education of children in the public elementary schools of the diocese, by establishing scholarships of from £5 to £10 annual value, to be held at some public elementary or superior school; and exhibitions of £50 annual value, to be held at some superior place of education. These scholarships and exhibitions are open to boys and girls who have attended for three years some public elementary school in the district.

The theological college of St. Bees, in the diocese

of Carlisle, was founded by Dr. Law, bishop of Chester, in the year 1816, and endowed by the Earl of Lonsdale with the incumbency of St. Bees. Its object is to supply a good and economical education for candidates for holy orders. The Bishop of Carlisle is the visitor.

SEAL OF THE PRIORY OF CARLISLE.

CHAPTER XII.

MISCELLANEA.

In looking over a list of the successors of Æthelwulf, in the see of Carlisle, one is struck by the large number that Cumberland and Westmorland can claim as their sons. The mediæval churchman of the South must have looked upon the offer of the see of Carlisle much as a modern one would look upon the offer of a bishopric in some remote and disagreeable colony,—perpetual banishment, if he did his duty, scant remuneration, the risk of having his residence burnt, or even of being killed; little wonder that no Italian prelate ever thought worth to come so far North for preferment. On the other hand there were some attractions to a man of ambition. The vicinity to Scotland necessarily made the bishop into a diplomatist of the first importance, and the confidential servant of his sovereign; while his education would give him the lead among the rude local barons with whom he would be associated in Scotch affairs. Carlisle can, spite of its disadvantages, boast that it has attracted every pattern of bishop but one: diplomatists, politicians, courtiers, soldiers, lawyers, scholars, and men of affairs, have all occupied the episcopal throne, but no bishop of the pattern of the mediæval saint has ever adorned the see of Carlisle. Rainbow was, perhaps, the nearest approach to one. Nicolson, of all the bishops that have ever reigned in Carlisle, was perhaps the one most suited for the see, as it was situated in the seventeenth and eighteenth centuries. A man of great personal strength, capable of riding enormous distances, and who thought nothing of preaching in the cathedral and of then walking out to Rose, who, as archdeacon, spent his holidays in hunting, and was not above taking an interest in a cock-fight: fond of a good dinner, a scholar, an antiquary, a linguist, ambitious and pushing, afraid of no one, a man who would have his own way, a native of the district, of high courage,[1] Nicolson was the very man to reduce to order the diocese, of which his "Primary Visitation"[2] records so painful a picture. His individuality comes out strongly, not only in the episcopal but in the political history of Carlisle. The other bishops of the eighteenth century present, as bishops, no individuality, though, apart from their episcopal positions, some of them were men of mark,—Lyttelton, President of the Society of Antiquaries of London; Douglas, scholar, Vice-president of the same society, Fellow of the Royal, and the friend of Johnson; and Goodenough,

---

[1] I gather these particulars from his unpublished journals: he went in his coach and six with the *posse comitatus* to confront the Highlanders in 1715, and when the Highlanders appeared, he was the only man who refused to run. He was carried unwillingly off the field by his coachman.

[2] *Ante*, p. 165.

(nineteenth century) famous for his botanical collections, Vice-President of the Royal and Linnæan Societies. The bishops of Carlisle, from Bradford, who succeeded Nicolson, down to Goodenough, were of the prevalent eighteenth-century type of bishop, good men and dignified, but somewhat apathetic in the conception and execution of their duties, as we now understand the duties of a bishop. With Goodenough's successors, the four last bishops of Carlisle, the courtly Percy, the aristocratic and unfortunate Villiers, the saintly Waldegrave, and the hard-working and energetic Goodwin, a new *régime* came in; the dry bones were made to live, churches were built, livings augmented, abuses reformed, religious and charitable organisations founded, and the diocese enlarged in 1856, on the death of Bishop Percy, and the duties and responsibilities of its overseer thereby, as in a hundred other ways, immensely augmented. If Harvey Goodwin (a name dear to all Cambridge men of the writer's standing) has not attained the fame as scholar, antiquary, or man of science, that some of his predecessors have done, it is not from lack of ability or inclination for the studies, but because of the devotedness with which he has given himself up to higher duties, a devotedness which has endeared him to the inhabitants of his diocese, who by nature are, of all men, the most cautious, the least given to gush, and most prone to be suspicious of one who has the misfortune to be *homo australis*, a man from the South. The writer, as one of that cautious, ungushing, and suspicious race, was himself somewhat surprised to see how the most unlikely people worked to make the Carlisle Church Congress of 1884 a success for the bishop's sake.

Of the priors of Carlisle we know little; a careful examination of the local monastic chartularies would probably add some names to the list and transfer one or two to Lanercost. Among the deans the most celebrated have had little connexion with the city from which they took their name. The deanery was secularised by Queen Elizabeth, and for long was held by laymen; in the seventeenth century it was a stepping-stone to other preferment, and if Dean Atterbury's name is associated with the deanery of Carlisle, it is in connexion with the quarrels of which he was great part. Dean Percy is famed for his "Reliques of English Poetry." It is among the nineteenth-century deans that we find the most illustrious,—Milner, president of Queen's, Cambridge; Tait, afterwards Archbishop of Canterbury, and Close; these three, in various ways, but particularly by their preaching and by their power of organising, did much to quicken religious life in Carlisle. There is no need here to further dilate upon such well-known churchmen.

Among the list of chancellors of the diocese which will be found in the county histories are some names which may be noted. Gregory Scott, vicar of St. Michael's, Bongate, Appleby, was the first person in the diocese of Carlisle to unite in himself the two offices of Official Principal and Vicar-General in Spirituals, which were as early as 1570, granted to him by letters patent from Bishop Barnes, who, probably, followed the form of letters patent under which he had himself been appointed chancellor of York by Archbishop Grindal.[1] These two offices together constitute the chancellorship, which at first was only granted by the bishops during pleasure. Bishop Meye in 1586 granted the chancellorship to Henry Dethick for life, and the grant was confirmed by the dean and chapter: this practice has been followed ever since. In 1622 Isaac Singleton was appointed to both the chancellorship and the archdeaconry of Carlisle. He died in 1643, and the chancellorship remained vacant until after the Restoration, while the seal of the office was lost during the Civil Wars. In 1661 Robert Lowther was appointed chancellor, and provided himself with a seal of office, on which he was represented sitting in a chair of state under a canopy and clad in the flowing robes and velvet cap of a doctor of the law. His successor, Henry Marshall, vicar of Stanwix, was murdered, in 1666, at the door of his vicarage under circumstances that are not recorded. To him succeeded Rowland Nicols, and then came, in 1683, Thomas Tullie, afterwards dean of Carlisle, who has already been heard of in connexion with "The Society for the Reformation of Manners." Tullie was

---

[1] While the Official Principal heard causes between party and party, and dealt usually with matters of *temporal* interest, such as marriages, wills, and the like, the Vicar-General exercised a jurisdiction only in spirituals, such as the correction of morals, granting institutions, preserving discipline, and so forth. See "Visitations in the Ancient Diocese of Carlisle." By J. E. Prescott, D.D., archdeacon of Carlisle. C. Thurnam & Sons. Carlisle: 1888. p. 27 *n*.

descended from a family of German miners that settled at Keswick in the time of Queen Elizabeth. One of them settled in Carlisle as a merchant, and his descendants became deans of Carlisle, Ripon, and York (subdean). Chancellor Tullie was succeeded, in 1727, by Chancellor Waugh, whose notebook has been made available for the purposes of this volume, and whose daughters, the "celebrated Miss Waughs of Carlisle," were long the leaders of an exclusive coterie in local society. Chancellor Waugh died in 1765, and was succeeded by Richard Burn, vicar of Orton in Westmorland. Like his predecessors, Lowther, Tullie, and Waugh, Burn was a native of the diocese, who, after being at Oxford, became, first, curate, and then, in 1736, vicar of Orton in Westmorland. Shortly after his appointment to the last office he was placed in the commission of the peace, and commenced to keep a notebook, in which he entered, under proper headings, all the information he could collect relative to the duties of a magistrate. This he was induced to publish, in 1754, under the title of " The Justice of the Peace and Parish Officer." The book had an enormous success, and is still a standard authority. Dr. Burn himself brought out fifteen editions of it, and at least as many more have appeared since his death. His other great work on " Ecclesiastical Law " was nearly as successful; it was published in 1763, and no doubt brought him under the notice of Dr. Lyttleton, who was appointed bishop of Carlisle in 1764, and who in the following year appointed Dr. Burn as his chancellor, an office which he held until his death in 1785.

He was the author, in conjunction with Joseph Nicolson, nephew of the bishop of that name, of "The History and Antiquities of Westmorland and Cumberland," a book which always commands a good high price, when it comes into the market. The next chancellor was the great Paley,[1] better known as archdeacon, a piece of preferment he held from 1782 to 1805. He was appointed chancellor in 1785, and resigned it in 1795, when he was succeeded by Joseph Dacre Carlyle, Professor of Arabic in the University of Cambridge, and perpetual curate of St. Cuthbert's, Carlisle, of which city he was a native. This distinguished Orientalist was selected, in 1799, to accompany Lord Elgin, who was sent in that year to the Ottoman Court as ambassador. Through Lord Elgin's influence, Chancellor Carlyle obtained admission to the libraries at Constantinople, and into those of the convents of Mount Athos, and in all these places he made catalogues of the works they contained. He travelled extensively in Asia Minor, Egypt, Syria, Greece, and Italy, and was the adviser of Lord Elgin in bringing home the marbles now known under that nobleman's name. He returned in 1801, after an absence of two years. He died in 1804, at the early age of 44, broken down by grief

---

[1] As it has been matter of controversy, it may be well to state that Paley lived in the abbey, in the house, now pulled down, belonging to his stall, the fourth; it was his widow and daughters who, after his death, lived in Paternoster-row. The writer received this information in 1881 from a venerable lady, who was on intimate terms with Dr. Paley and his family, and a near relation to his second wife.

at the loss of his only son, for whom he had entertained great ambitions, and by the fatigues of his travels. He published, in 1796, some specimens of Arabic poetry, and after his death a volume of poems by him was published. He was the author of a hymn, which a great authority calls "almost perfect":—

> "Lord, when we bend before Thy throne,
> And our *confessions* pour,
> Teach us to feel the sins we own,
> And hate what we deplore." [1]

Dr. Brown Grisdale next held the chancellorship, from 1804 to his death in 1814, when he was succeeded by his son-in-law, Walter Fletcher, vicar of Dalston and prebendary of York. On his death, in 1846, he was succeeded by Dr. Jackson, rector of Lowther, who retained it until 1855, when he vacated it on acceptance of the archdeaconry of Carlisle, which he vacated on becoming Provost of Queen's College, Oxford.

The Rev. C. J. Burton was appointed chancellor of Carlisle in 1855 by Bishop Percy, and retained the office until his death, in 1887, at the advanced age of ninety-five, with his intellectual faculties in no way impaired by his weight of years. No greater lawyer ever sat upon the bench, and some of his early judgments in matrimonial causes, before his

---

[1] "Poems," by the late J. D. Carlyle, chancellor of Carlisle, &c. London: White, Fleet-street. 1805, p. 141. See also "Christian Hymns and Hymn-writers," by J. E. Prescott, archdeacon of Carlisle. Cambridge: Deighton & Co. 1883. p. 154

court was deprived of the jurisdiction, are masterpieces, particularly his remarks on the mischievous results of the Scotch marriage laws so far as it affected the morality of the northern counties of England.[1] His action had much to do with bringing about a great and beneficial change in the law.

On the death of Chancellor Burton the office was conferred by Bishop Goodwin, for the first time in its history, on a layman, who is, by the way, a native of and resident in the diocese. Advantage was also taken of the opportunity to put on a more usual footing the relations between the chancellor and the archdeacon of Carlisle, which had long been of an anomalous character.

For many years prior to 1887, under the supposed authority of letters patent granted him by the bishop, the chancellor of the diocese has cited the clergy and the churchwardens, and has held, from time to time, what of late has been called a visitation. The bishop, as a rule, has visited every third year, and has then inhibited both the archdeacon and the chancellor. The usual explanation given was that given by Chancellor Burn in his "Ecclesiastical Law" and his "History of Westmorland and Cumberland," namely, that the archdeacon had sold his visitatorial jurisdiction for a pension. The matter has been gone into most thoroughly by the present able and accurate holder of the dignity in his primary charge

[1] During the week of Carlisle hiring, the average number of marriages celebrated at one well-known house at Gretna was a hundred, all the parties being, almost without exception, farm servants.

to the clergy and churchwardens of his archdeaconry. He explodes the notion handed down by chancellor Burn, and comes to the following conclusion :—

"The whole story seems to be perfectly plain. By a composition with the Bishop, the general or fixed Court of the Archdeacon was united with the Diocesan Court, the Archdeacon's power of Visitation and his Visitation Court being retained, and the money consideration for synodals, court fees and fines being paid to him by the Bishop. The difficulty both of travelling and of raising his Procurations becoming very great, the Archdeacon's Visitations became less frequent, and gradually fell into abeyance. Meanwhile, the Bishop's Official Principal held General Chapters, at different centres *every year*, for the correction of morals and other legal business. These General Chapters, in the years when the Bishop did not visit, assumed at length, in the last century, irregularly, the name and character of a Visitation. But this was under no definite authority, either from the Bishop or as inherent in the office of Chancellor."[1]

Various changes in the ecclesiastical law deprived the ecclesiastical courts of much, nay, of most of their jurisdiction.

"The result has been the gradual, but practical, extinction of the general archidiaconal court, though it still legally exists, and the reduction of the jurisdiction of the chancellor in the diocesan court to little more than the granting of faculties. The position, then, of the archdeacon of Carlisle, say some sixty years ago, was reduced to this,—the power of inducting clergy who had been instituted by the bishop, the right, not often

---

[1] "Visitation in the Ancient Diocese of Carlisle." By J. E. Prescott, D.D., archdeacon of Carlisle. C. Thurnam & Sons. Carlisle: 1888. p. 29. This is a mine of information on local history, and to it this volume is much indebted.

exercised, of presenting candidates for ordination, and the occasional visiting of parochial churches."[1]

The addition of a new archdeaconry to the diocese in 1856 created further complication, and the two archdeacons of the diocese arranged with Chancellor Burton to hold visitations as his surrogates. On the resignation of Archdeacon Jackson in 1863, and the death of Archdeacon Evans in 1865, Chancellor Burton took upon himself the visitations in both archdeaconries. Legal proceedings were commenced against him, but were not prosecuted to a decision: the question was allowed to slumber during the lifetime of Chancellor Burton. On his death, in 1887, Bishop Goodwin took all the steps in his power to make the jurisdiction of three of his archdeacons in all respects as in other dioceses, and modified the letters patent of the new chancellor by the removal of a clause as to synods and chapters, which had been relied upon as giving the chancellor power to hold visitations. The archdeacons held their first visitation in 1888.

The name of Paley sheds lustre on the archdeaconry of Carlisle, an office which has frequently been in the eighteenth century the stepping-stone to a deanery or bishopric, in three cases to the bishopric of Carlisle. The rectory of Great Salkeld was, from very early date, attached to the archdeaconry of Carlisle, but when the archdeaconry was endowed with a canonry at Carlisle, the living passed into the patronage of the bishop under an Order in Council,

[1] "Visitation in the Ancient Diocese of Carlisle," p. 31.

dated May 1st, 1855. This Order saved the canonry in question from being suppressed by a bill introduced into Parliament by the late Mr. Ferguson, of Morton, at the instigation of a large body of his constituents, who were desirous to devote its income to the augmentation of the poor livings in Carlisle. The bill was read a second time, when the bishop and the Ecclesiastical Commissioners intervened, bringing down on their heads the wrath of the *Times*.

The lists of the prebendaries of Carlisle include many names that have already been presented to notice as archdeacons, chancellors, deans, and bishops of Carlisle; others have found preferment elsewhere, like Sandys, in succession bishop of Worcester and London and archbishop of York; John Law, bishop of Elphin; George Law, bishop in succession of Chester and of Bath and Wells. The celebrated John Emamuel Tremellius, professor of Hebrew at Cambridge, held a prebend at Carlisle in the sixteenth century. Arthur Savage, prebendary from 1660 to 1700, was a great benefactor to the chapter. Hugh Todd, in succession vicar of Stanwix, rector of Arthuret, and vicar of Penrith, is perhaps the best known of all the prebendaries of Carlisle; a man of great ability and scholarship, who has been handed down to fame by the many controversies he was mixed up in, some of which have already been alluded to. He was the compiler of sundry manuscript local histories, about whom there has always been a savour of mystery and controversy. He, Savage, and Bishop Smith founded the present chapter library at

Carlisle. Joseph Hudson, prebendary from 1782 to 1811, was sprung from a family of statesmen (yeomen) near Caldbeck, and educated at Glasgow. As curate of Highhead, near Dalston, he took an active part in the great enclosures of the commons in Cumberland, and earned the name of the *Pasture priest*. His skill in decyphering ancient documents enabled him to render great assistance to the Duke of Portland in his celebrated litigation with Sir James Lowther, for which he was rewarded with the promise of an Irish bishopric, but this preferment he exchanged with Dr. John Law for a stall in Carlisle cathedral, and the vicarages of Newburn and Warkworth in Northumberland. Many stories are told of his eccentricities : he was ambitious of adding to his honours the archdeaconry of Carlisle, and employed all the political influence he could bring to that end. On hearing that Dr. Paley was appointed, the disappointed canon retired to his study and (so says his journal) prayed for the new archdeacon.

The prebendaries of Carlisle were at one time far from popular in their cathedral city : Whigs when the citizens were Tory, Tory when the citizens were Radicals, their meddling in the parliamentary elections, a pernicious legacy from Bishop Nicolson, was resented. Dean Tait put an end to the system, though Dean Close used now and then to urge his friends to vote for Sir Wilfrid Lawson. Better feelings prevail, and it will be long ere the good work done on the school board of Carlisle by the late lamented Canon Chalker will be forgotten in that city.

Coming to the parochial clergy, allusion has already been made to the influence wielded by the Rev. John Fawcett, perpetual incumbent of St. Cuthbert's, Carlisle, far beyond that ever attained by any other incumbent in the diocese. Among the many earnest and generous lay churchmen in the diocese, the name of the late George Moore stands prominently to the front.

SEAL OF CHANCELLOR LOWTHER.

CHAPTER XIII.

ARCHÆOLOGICAL.

THE ecclesiastical architecture of the diocese of Carlisle has been influenced by the circumstances under which that diocese has existed;—its dangerous proximity to Scotland; its liability during great part of its existence to devastating raids; its consequent poverty; and its lack of wealthy traders in wool and wine, such as reared the glorious churches of Lincolnshire. The diocese of Carlisle lacks such churches; its cathedral is but small, less even when uninjured than several parish churches in other dioceses, and now a fragment only of itself: a native of the diocese can have no idea of what church or cathedral can be until he has travelled beyond its limits.

The earliest ecclesiastical building we have record of in the land of Carlisle is in the *Veredictum Antiquorum*, somewhere between 1056 and 1071, preserved in the cartulary of Lanercost, concerning the chapel of Triermaine, in Gilsland. It says the lord of Triermain *fecit primum unam capellam de virgis*, a chapel of wattlework. It is probable that most of the churches in this diocese were originally of this material, and that they were gradually replaced by buildings of stone after the advent of the Norman into the diocese, though in some cases the change may have been sooner.

The earliest type of church of stone in the diocese is to be found at Over Denton, near where the Roman Wall enters Cumberland from Northumberland, the quarry from which the church was built. This church retains its original plan, unaltered except that the west end has been rebuilt: it consists of chancel and nave, the chancel being only 11 ft. wide and 12 ft. long and the nave 27 ft. by 16 ft. wide: the original chancel arch remains. The nave possesses two doorways, the principal one, that to the south, is square headed, the lintel being supported on two quaintly-wrought corbels; that to the north is built up. One of the original windows remains on the north side, a round-headed slit, only a few inches wide, made before the general use of glass, and therefore kept as small as possible. The other windows are insertions of various dates. The west wall and belfry are modern, but built on the old foundations. In the absence of detail, it is difficult to fix the date of this church: the peculiar form of the door, and the rude character of the chancel arch, resembling that under the tower at Corbridge, have induced some to believe that Over Denton Church may be an example of that primitive English Romanesque called Saxon, but it is more generally assigned to early Norman Romanesque. The ground plan of Over Denton church is that from which most of the parish churches in the diocese of Carlisle were developed: the general process being, first, the lengthening, in Norman times, of short Norman chancels, as at Dacre and Torpenhow; then followed the widening of the nave by the addition on the north side of an aisle, as at Ormside, Dacre, Torpenhow, Irthington, Blencogo, Dearham, and the subsequent addition in many instances of a south aisle also; the addition of a tower at the west end, sometimes as at Ormside, built to abut on the west wall with only a door of communication, but more usually as at Caldbeck, built to the west of the existing church, and the nave lengthened to meet it by an additional arch to its arcades; next, the addition of a clerestory and large windows, as the use of glass became more general; the further rebuilding on a larger scale of some part of the building, a process which went on to post-reformation times; at Ormside we find the chancel rebuilt on a larger scale; and finally the introduction of the ugly modern sash window. The church of Over Denton, owing to the poverty of the parish, and the paucity of inhabitants, escaped these improvements, and, carefully repaired as it has been under skilled advice, enables us to see the original germ from which the parish churches of the diocese have grown. Two or three of its neighbours also escaped until the end of the last or beginning of this century, when they were pulled down, in whole or part, and replaced by hideous and shapeless erections, covered with a coating of roughcast.

Among the churches of the diocese that have had a continuous life, many very interesting ones exist. Some of the churches in the diocese of Carlisle are fortresses as well as churches, being intended as refuges for the inhabitants in times of hostile raids: such are those of Burgh-on-Sands, Newton Arlosh, Great Salkeld, and others whose towers are places of strength; the abbey of Holm Cultram was protected by heavy earthworks, and the inhabitants of the parish, in a petition to Cromwell in 1538, ask for his intercession with the king to keep the church standing as a "greate ayde, socor, and defence for us agenst our neghbours the Scots." Another tell-tale feature of the churches in the old diocese of Carlisle is their modesty; they are generally placed in a valley, and the tower rises just to the level of the surrounding hills, so that a watcher on the top may see any one that crosses these hills, while the tower itself is not conspicuous, and does not catch the eye of any wandering marauder from Scotland. Such is the tower of Dearham; such was that of Wetheral until modern ingenuity placed a sort of summer-house on its top. The antiquary will be interested in the church of Bolton, Cumberland, with its pointed barrel roof of stone, ascribed by local legend to Michael Scott, the wizard; in the church of Warwick, with its circular apse; of Torpenhow, with its fine chancel arch, and its unique classical ceiling, painted with cupids and flowers; Long Marton, with its curiously-carved tympanum: in fact, most of the parish churches that have had a continuous life possess some feature over which the antiquary will love to linger and to speculate.

A few larger churches exist in the old diocese of Carlisle,—at Appleby, Kirkby Stephen, Brough-on-

Stainmoor, Crosthwaite (Keswick), Caldbeck, Greystoke, &c., mostly Perpendicular in style, but, as a rule, somewhat poor and bald. The district added to the diocese in 1856, possesses fine large churches at Kendal, Kirkby Lonsdale, and Ulverstone.

The last century saw some commodious Georgian churches erected at Carlisle, Penrith, Wigton, Workington, and Whitehaven. It has always been the fashion to abuse these churches; they are ugly without, inside they are comfortable and convenient, and capable, when well treated, like St. Cuthbert's, Carlisle, of being made very beautiful. One can hardly commend the attempt now being made to convert the one at Workington, built in 1780, into a Gothic church, inside and outside. At Kirkandrews-on-Esk is a fine building of red sandstone, with a tower and spire in the classic manner, but bald and poor inside, built from the designs of Telford, the great road engineer, and standing north and south, an eccentricity which was purposely exceeded in Christ Church and Trinity Church, Carlisle, built in 1830, and St. John's, Houghton, built in 1840: these churches have a tower at the east end, and the altar at their west. Good work in churches has been done in the last two episcopates, and it may be said that on the whole the churches of this diocese have been fortunate in their repairs; the churches of Isel and Burgh-by-Sands may be quoted as an example. Of modern churches several good examples exist. The new church of St. Nicholas, Whitehaven, and those at Millum, Dalton-in-Furness, and Netherton, are, perhaps, the most noteworthy.

The diocese has more to boast of, architecturally, in the remains of its great religious foundations. In Carlisle Cathedral the Norman work in the fragmentary nave, the beautiful early English aisles, the noble east window of Decorated date, the doom in painted glass in the top thereof, the unique series of carvings on the capitals of the chancel pillars, representing the labours of the months, the legendary paintings on the backs of the stalls, and the carved woodwork (of which, alas, too little is left) are all of the highest interest. Want of space forbids us from entering into a detailed account and history of Carlisle Cathedral, but the following table may be useful:—

CARLISLE CATHEDRAL.

Building commenced, reign of William Rufus...	*post* 1092
A priory of Austin Canons established there ...	1102
A bishop's seat established there	1133
Choir taken down and enlarged, &c.	1245–1255
Burnt	1292
Rebuilt	1352–1362
Stained glass inserted in east window	1380–1384
Transept partly burnt	1392
Upper part of tower built	1401
Stalls erected	1401
Legendary paintings added...	1484
The Priory surrendered to the Crown	1540
Dean and Chapter created	1541
Nave and chapter-house destroyed	1645–1646
Ancient ceiling, bishop's throne, &c., destroyed	1764
Restored...	1855

Little remains of the Benedictine Priory at Wetheral beyond the gateway tower, but careful search might reveal a good deal; the ruins are said to have been used by the canons of Carlisle as a quarry when they built their residential houses shortly after 1660.

Of the church of the once great and wealthy Cistercian Abbey of Holm Cultram all that remains is a most melancholy fragment of the nave; every evil that can be imagined has befallen this luckless church, which in length exceeded the cathedral of Carlisle in its best days; it has been burnt by fire; the steeple was blown over by the winds to the ruination of the chancel and transepts; parts were rebuilt and pulled down by the parishioners, until nothing but the six westernmost bays of the nave remained, and of these the parishioners pulled down the aisles, and with the materials walled up the nave arcades. A fine transitional western door, covered by a modern porch, tells of the former splendours of the Abbey of Holm Cultram, and the farm-houses of the district are replete with carvings in stone and wood obtained from too ready a quarry. Part of the monastic buildings, the mill, and the boundaries of the precincts can yet be made out, and legends of the grandeur of the great abbot, Robert Chamber, and of his white horses still linger. This abbey was founded in 1150 by Prince Henry, son of David, King of Scotland; its revenues were valued at £477. 19s. 3d. in the *Valor* of Henry VIII. Queen Mary granted the rectory of Holm Cultram, the advowson of the vicarage, and all tithes and other profits and emoluments of the rectory and church of Holm Cultram, and the chapel at Newton Arlosh to the University of Oxford. The abbot was also lord of the great manor of Holm Cultram, co-extensive with the parish; this the Crown took, and long did the parishioners have cause to regret the change, and fierce and prolonged was the litigation that arose.

But if the wreck of Holm Cultram inspires the spectator with melancholy, the beauty and vivacity of ruined Lanercost will do much to raise the spirits again. Beautifully situated in a charming valley on the north side of the river Irthing, in a commanding position, whence two long reaches of water lead the eye to the Roman stations of Nether Denton and Walton, the ruins of this house of Austin Canons is the architectural gem of the diocese, enriched by a setting of most lovely scenery, in striking contrast with the sterile moors and barren fells over which the neighbouring Roman Wall pursues its course. This house was founded in 1169 by Robert de Vallibus, baron of Gilsland. We have already incidentally in this volume made mention of the sufferings it endured from Scotch invasions, and raids; of the visits paid to it by Edward I., and of the poverty and obscurity into which it fell. The greater part of the buildings now remaining are of the very best period of the Early English architecture of the thirteenth century, and we may see at once that little of the structure was raised in 1169. The income of the priory as given in the *Valor* of Henry VIII., was only £77. 11s. 11d. Most of the property of the dissolved house was granted by Henry VIII. and Edward VI. to Sir Thomas Dacre the Bastard, who converted some of the domestic buildings into a dwelling-house. The nave now forms a beautiful parish church, a purpose for which it originally served, the church being, as at Carlisle, a divided one, but in the last century the nave was roofless, and the parish church was held in the north aisle.

Hardly inferior in beauty of site and interest is the Premonstratensian house at Shap, whose ruins are nestled into a charming little valley amid bleak Westmorland fells. This house was founded about the end of the twelfth century, and the buildings were commenced shortly after that date, and went on almost continuously until near the dissolution, when the revenues were valued at £154. 17s. 7½d. The possessions were granted to the Whartons, and now are in the Lowthers.

There are some religious houses in the district, added to the diocese in 1856, which must be briefly mentioned, though their histories belong to the history of the archdeaconry of Richmond, to the histories of the sees of York and Chester.

At St. Bees, probably on or near the site of the nunnery established by St. Bega and destroyed by the Danes, a fine church commemorates the Benedictine Priory which William le Meschines founded while Thurstan was archbishop of York (1119–1139), as a cell of St. Mary's, York. In the *Valor* of Henry VIII. its revenues were estimated at £143. 16s. 2d., surpassed only in the county of Cumberland by St. Mary's, Carlisle, and Holm Cultram. Its possessions passed to the Chaloners, and through the Wyberghs to the Lowthers.

Seven miles to the south of St. Bees the Cistercians had a house at Calder, founded about 1130 by Ranulp le Meschin, son of the founder of St. Bees, whose beautiful ruins may almost compare with those of Lanercost. It was valued in the *Valor* of Henry VIII. at £50. 9s. 3½d., and the site of the abbey was granted to Dr. Thomas Leigh. The church is now in ruins, but part of the domestic buildings have been converted into a dwelling-house.

A little Benedictine nunnery existed at Seton, in south-west Cumberland. Its revenues only amounted to £12. 12s. 0½d.; and we have omitted to mention a little Benedictine nunnery at Armathwaite, on the river Eden, which had a revenue, after paying their chaplain, of £13. 12s.

In the portion of Lancashire which was added to the diocese of Carlisle in 1856,—viz., Lancashire North of the Sands—were the great Cistercian house of Furness, with an income of £805. 16s. 5d.; the Austin Canons' priories of Conishead, £97. 9s. 11d., and of Cartmel, £91. 6s. 3d. Of Conishead little remains; the church of Cartmel and the ruins of Furness are well known.

No remains exist of the houses of the *quatuor ordines* of friars at Carlisle, Appleby, and Penrith; nor of the leper hospitals at Carlisle, Appleby, and Kendal. There were several small chantries in the diocese, but only one, that of St. Alban's, Carlisle, existed as a separate building, and it now survives in the name of a street.

An elaborate catalogue and account of the church plate of the diocese has been compiled and published by the local Archæological Society.[1] Only one example of pre-Reformation church plate is known in the diocese (we now speak of the extended diocese), a chalice of the middle of the fourteenth century, at Old Hutton, near Kendal. A Communion cup, with cover of secular work, at Bridekirk, comes next in date,—viz., 1550-1. The Communion cups of Great Salkeld and Crosthwaite (Westmorland), both of the year 1567-8, both of York make, and one at Newton Reigny, 1568-9, come next. Five cups of 1570-1 and eleven of 1571-2 are historically interesting, as closely following upon the appointment of Bishop Barnes to the see of Carlisle, who seems to have enforced the injunctions about Communion cups of Archbishop Grindal, whose chancellor he had been. There are in the diocese thirty-nine more cups of Elizabethan date, twenty-three of London make, three of York, three of unknown assay, and ten assigned to an irregular assay at Carlisle. Of post-Elizabethan plate, in the seventeenth century, the diocese contains ninety-eight examples, fifty-seven from London, twenty from York, nine from Newcastle-on-Tyne, eight doubtful, while Dublin, Hull, Nuremberg, and Cartagena each contribute a single example. The diocese possesses fifty-six examples of the Britannia or higher-class silver, of which forty-three are from London, twelve from Newcastle, and one from Chester. One peculiarity should be noticed, the rarity of silver Communion flagons,

[1] "Old Church Plate in the Diocese of Carlisle," Cumberland and Westmorland Archæological and Antiquarian Society. C. Thurnam, Carlisle, 1888.

especially in Cumberland, down to recent times. Only four parish churches in Cumberland, twelve in Westmorland, and two in the part of Lancashire now belonging to the diocese of Carlisle, had silver flagons before the nineteenth century, and only four, all in Westmorland, had such before the eighteenth. The earlier flagons were all of pewter.

Edward VI.'s commissioners, though ordered to allow only one bell to remain at each church, seem not to have strictly, if at all, followed their instructions in this respect throughout Cumberland and Westmorland, since to this day several churches in these counties retain at least two bells, which, by their shape, stamps, and legends, are clearly shown to have survived from mediæval times; the most noteworthy instance being Greystoke, the only Cumberland church besides the cathedral which had "foure gret belles" in 1552, which same four it still retains. The "quatuor magnæ campanæ," given by Bishop Strickland, in 1401, to the cathedral, remained intact until three of them were recast in 1658. The churches of Burgh-by-Sands, Renwick, Distington, Dacre, and Edenhall have each two pre-Reformation bells, as also had Skelton church, when visited by Bishop Nicolson in 1703.

Few Cumberland churches, according to Edward VI.'s inventory, had more than two bells in 1552; and wherever, as at Holm Cultram, Cumrew, Scaleby, Langwathby, Aikton, Newton Reigny, Castle Sowerby, Egremont, Eskdale, Brigham, Ennerdale, Threlkeld, &c., only one mediæval bell remains, it can, in most of these cases, be shown that its mate disappeared in the last century. As yet the church bells of this diocese, mostly hung in gable-cots, and therefore difficult of access, have been but partially explored. But, from the discoveries which are being made, there is reason to believe that the diocese contains a larger percentage of ancient bells than any other part of England; and, as many of them are of considerable antiquarian interest, it is to be hoped that they may escape the fate which, in these days of "restoration," too often befals the venerable relics of the past in our parish churches.

SEAL OF CUSTODIAN OF SPIRITUALITIES OF THE DIOCESE OF CARLISLE, SEDE VACANTE.

SUCCESSION OF THE BISHOPS OF CARLISLE.

		ACCESSION.[1]
1.	Æthelwulf	1133
2.	Bernard	1156

He died in 1186. After his death the see was vacant until 1218, during a part of which time the revenues and custody of the see were granted to a foreign archbishop.

3.	Hugh	1218
4.	Walter Malclerk, *res.*	1223
5.	Silvester de Everdon	1246
*6.	Thomas Vipont	1255
7.	Robert de Chauncy	1256
*8.	Ralph de Irton	1280
*9.	John de Halton?	1292
10.	John de Ross	1325
11.	John de Kirby	1332
	John de Horncastle,[2] *dep.*	1352
*12.	Gilbert de Welton?	1353
*13.	Thomas de Appleby?	1362
*14.	Robert Reed? *trans.*	1396
15.	Thomas Merks, *dep.*	1397
*16.	William Strickland	1400
*17.	Robert Whelpdale	1419
18.	William Barrow	1422

---

[1] The date of the consecration and of the restitution of the temporalities are sometimes much later than the date of the accession—often a year, sometimes two—which occasions much confusion.

[2] This ecclesiastic had possession of the see and restitution of the temporalities, but seems to never have been consecrated, and so is not generally reckoned among the bishops of Carlisle.

SUCCESSION OF BISHOPS.

19.	Marmaduke Lumley, *trans.*	1429
20.	Nicholas Close, *trans.*	1449
21.	William Percy	1452
22.	John Kingscote	1462
23.	Richard Scrope	1463
*24.	Edward Story ?, *trans.*	1468
25.	Richard Bell	1477
26.	William Sever, *trans.*	1496
*27.	Roger Leyburn	1502
28.	John Penny	1508
29.	John Kite	1501
30.	Robert Oldridge, or Aldridge	1537
31.	Owen Oglethorpe	1556
32.	John Best	1560
33.	Richard Barnes, *trans.*	1570
34.	John Meye	1577
*35.	Henry Robinson	1598
36.	Robert Snowden	1616
*37.	Richard Milburn	1621
*38.	Richard Senhouse	1622
39.	Francis White, *trans.*	1626
*40.	Barnaby Potter	1628
41.	James Usher	1641

A vacancy from 1656.

42.	Richard Sterne, *trans.*	1660
43.	Edward Rainbow	1664
*44.	Thomas Smith	1684
*45.	William Nicolson, *trans.*	1702
46.	Samuel Bradford, *trans.*	1718
*47.	John Waugh	1723
*48.	Sir George Fleming	1734
49.	Richard Osbaldiston, *trans.*	1747
50.	Charles Lyttleton	1764
*51.	Edmund Law	1768
52.	John Douglas, *trans.*	1787
53.	Edward Venables Vernon [Harcourt], *trans.*	1791
54.	Samuel Goodenough	1808
55.	Hugh Percy	1827

56. Henry Montague Villiers, *trans.* 1856
57. Samuel Waldegrave............................. 1860
58. HARVEY GOODWIN............................. 1869

Bishops marked with an asterisk (fourteen in number) are natives of the diocese of Carlisle, as it now (1888) exists. Those marked with an asterisk and queried (five in number) are most probably natives of the diocese. Several others are north countrymen; others held preferment in the diocese before they became bishops thereof. With the possible exceptions of the second and third, the bishops of Carlisle have all been Englishmen.

BISHOP OF BARROW-IN-FURNESS.

1. HENRY WARE 1889

PRIORS OF CARLISLE.

This list cannot be relied upon. See *ante*, p. 208.

Athelwald
Walter
John
Bartholmew
Ralph
Robert de Morville
Adam de Helton
Allan
John de Halton
John de Kendall
Robert
Adam de Warthwic
William de Hautwyssell
Robert de Helperton
Simon de Hautwyssell
William de Hastworth
John de Kirby
Galfrid
John de Horncastle
Richard de Rydale
John de Penrith
William de Dalston
Robert de Edenhall
Thomas de Hoton
Thomas Elye
Thomas Barnaby
Thomas Haithwaite
Thomas Gondibour
Simon Senhouse
Christopher Slee
Lancelot Salkeld

DEANS OF CARLISLE.

With the years in which they were respectively installed.

1. Lancelot Salkeld, A.D. 1542
   The last prior and first dean.
2. Sir Thomas Smith, LL.D. 1560
3. Sir John Wooley, knight, M.A. 1577
4. Christopher Perkins, LL.D. 1596
5. Francis White, S.T.P., preferred to Bishop of Carlisle 1622
6. William Paterson, S.T.P., Dean of Exeter 1626
7. Thomas Comber, S.T.P. 1630
8. Guy Carleton, D.D., Bishop of Bristol and Chichester 1660
9. Thomas Smith, D.D., Bishop of Carlisle 1671
10. Thomas Musgrave, D.D. 1684
11. William Graham, D.D., Dean of Wells 1686
12. Francis Atterbury, D.D., Bishop of Rochester, &c. 1704
13. George Smalridge, D.D., Dean of Christchurch ... 1711
14. Thomas Gibson, D.D. 1713
15. Thomas Tullie, LL.D. 1716
16. Sir George Fleming, Bart., LL.D., Bishop of Carlisle 1727
17. Robert Bolton, LL.D. 1734
18. Charles Tarrent, LL.D., Dean of Peterborough 1764
19. Thomas Wilson, D.D. 1764
20. Thomas Percy, D.D., Bishop of Dromore 1778
21. Jeffrey Ekins, D.D. 1782
22. Isaac Milner, D.D., F.R.S. 1792
23. Robert Hodgson, D.D., F.R.S. 1820
24. John Anthony Cramer, D.D. 1844
25. Samuel Hinds, D.D., Bishop of Norwich 1848
26. A. C. Tait, D.D., D.C.L., Archbishop of Canterbury 1850
27. Francis Close, D.D. 1856
28. John Oakley, D.D., Dean of Manchester 1881
29. W. G. Henderson, D.D., D.C.L. 1884

INDEX.

---o---

ÆTHELFRITH takes Chester, 29
ÆTHELWALD or ÆTHELWULF, 66, 68, 72
—— charters by, 67
Æthelwulf, prior of Carlisle, 66, 67, 71
Agricola, 11, 12, 13
Alberic the legate, 68
ALDRIDGE, see OLDRIDGE
Alfred the Great, 44
Allen, Rev. M., 184
Alston : why not in diocese of Carlisle, 3
Altar tables, east and west, 165
Andrew, St., dedications to, 53
APPLEBY, THOMAS DE, 95
Architecture, ecclesiastical, in Carlisle diocese, 219
Archdeaconries, the, 186, 215
Archdeacon, relations between the Chancellor and the, 213
Archdeacon of Carlisle, his official, 77
Ardderyd, battle of, 35
Armathwaite, nunnery at, 65, 228
Armyne, William de, elected bishop of Carlisle, 90
Arthur, King, 29
Aske's Rebellion, 111
Aspatria, assarts out of parish of, become parishes, 80
Atterbury, Dr., dean of Carlisle, 166, 167, 168, 169

Audland, John, 140, 141
Augustine, St., 24, 36
Augustinian Canons at Carlisle, 66, 68
Australis homo, the, 90, 207

BALDER, 55
Baldwin, Rev. Roger, 152
Baptists, Carlisle, their pastor, 143
Barlow, bishop of Lincoln, 201
BARNES, RICHARD, 121, 125, 140
—— injunctions as to vestments, 125
—— enforces Grindal's injunctions as to cup and chalices, 125
—— visits the Cathedral, 126
Barri, Radulf, prior of Carlisle, 73
Barrow, St. George's Vicarage, 3
BARROW, WILLIAM, 104
Beckermet cross shaft, 57
Bees, St., theological college at, 204
—— priory at, 227
Bega, St., 32
—— nunnery of, 32, 54
Bell, John, Q.C., 202
BELL, RICHARD, 105
Bells, church, in diocese of Carlisle, 230
Beltain fires, 22
Benedict Biscop, 31
Benedictines at Wetheral, 68
Benson, Gervaise, 141, 144

Benson, Rev. George, 146
Bequests to local bridges and to the cathedral, 97
BERNARD, 69, 72
—— charters by, 70
Bernard, archbishop of Ragusa, 70
—— —— Sclavonia, 70
BEST, JOHN, 121, 122, 123, 125
Bewcastle Cross, 57
Bible Society, the, 190
Bishops of Carlisle, characteristics of, 205
"Black Book," the, 110
Blain, Rev. Joseph, 184
Boisil, 31
Bolton, Robert, dean of Carlisle, 172
Borrowdale, Abbot Gawen, surrenders Holm Cultram, 113
Boutflower Memorial Fund, 193
BRADFORD, SAMUEL, 171, 207
Braithwaite, Rev. George, a supposed centenarian, 178, 182
Brampton Church in 1704, 175
Bridekirk, Font, 57
Bridget, St., dedications to, 32
Brigantes, the, and their cities, 10
Bronze implements, 7
Bruce, Robert, swears fealty to Edward I. in Carlisle Cathedral, 85
—— stabs John Comyn, 86
—— cursed in Carlisle Cathedral, 87
—— wastes Cumberland, 88
—— Edward, wastes Cumberland, 88
Brythons, the, 8
Buchanan, Rev. George, 146
Burn, chancellor, 171, 210
Burnand, Rev. Nathaniel, 139, 152, 153
Burrough, Edward, 141
Burton, chancellor, 200, 212
Burton, dean of Kildare, 201

CAERLAVEROCK Castle, 80
Cæsar: his account of Britain, 9
Calder Abbey, 228
Camm, John, 141
Candida Casa, 23
—— bishops of, 64, 69, 76
Candlesticks, 163
Canon, Rev. Thomas, 146
Canons, minor, suspected of papism: how punished, 126
—— minor, kicking and boxing, 169
Carleton Guy, dean of Carlisle, 146
Carilef, William de St., bishop of Durham, 64
Carlisle, 18, 29
—— attacked in Aske's Rebellion, 111
—— besieged by William the Lion, 70
—— canons of, revolt, 71
—— corporation of, gives donations to preachers and ministers, 137
—— —— move their chapel, 137
—— Dean and Chapter, created, 114
—— endowed, 114
—— deanery secularised, 121, 208
—— defended by Andrew de Hercla, 88
—— destroyed by fire, 81
—— diocese of, boundaries, 1
—— —— archdeaconries, 2
—— —— rural deaneries, 2
—— —— patronage in, 3
—— —— endowments of, 69, 72, 108, 121
—— —— long vacant, 71
—— —— impoverished, 90, 93
—— —— improved condition in 1747, 172
—— —— fees on translations to, 108

Carlisle diocese, clergy of, in 1561, 122
—— —— clergy of, in 1563, 123
—— —— 1703-4, 165
—— —— miscellany accounts of, 165
—— —— granted to St. Cuthbert, 40
—— House at Lambeth Marsh, 109
—— invested by Earl of Buchan, 84
—— land of, 59
—— land of, severed from Durham, 65
—— —— made part of England, 49
—— —— made English ground, 31
—— laid waste, 44
—— St. Mary's Priory surrendered, 114
—— monastery at, 65
—— nunnery and schools at, 54
—— order as to alderman attending church, 136
—— priors of, 71
—— rebuilt by William II., 49
—— siege of, 1644, 138
—— St. Cuthbert's Church, 41, 51, 52
—— St. Mary's Church, 52
—— the aborigines of, in 1797, 188
Carlyle, chancellor, 202, 211
Cartmell Priory, 228
Cathedral, account of, 224
—— account of, in 1634, 134
—— founded, 114
—— buildings, pulled down, 138
—— Carlisle, in 1687, 162
—— of Carlisle a divided church, 66
—— school, 139
—— statutes litigation, 115
Celts, the, 6
Chalker, Canon, 217

Chancellors, 208
—— relations between, and the archdeacons, 213
Chapels used as schoolhouses, 181
Chapel, or pew, the Mayor's, 137, 139
Chapelries, the, 173, 179, 180, 181
Charles II., death of, 154
Chartularies, the monastic, 102
CHAUNCEY, ROBERT DE, 62, 76, 77, 78
Cheham, John de, bishop of Glasgow, 62
Chester, capture of, 29
Christian, bishop of Candida Casa, 69
Christianity in Roman times, 22
Churches, early type of, 220
—— growth of, 221
—— fortified, 222
—— Perpendicular, 222
—— Georgian, 223
—— recent, 223
—— with altar at west end, 223
—— standing north and south, 223
Church Extension Society, the Carlisle Diocesan, 192
—— extension, the diocese, 193
—— and dissent, relations between, 190
—— and dissent, Bishop Nicolson on, 159
—— and dissent acting together, Bishop Smith on, 161
—— goods, inventory of, 1562, 116
—— Missionary Society, 191
Cistercians at Holm Cultram, 69
Clergy Aid Society, Carlisle Diocesan, 192
Clerical incomes in 18th century, 174, 175, 176, 177, 178, 179
—— training fund, diocesan, 193
Close, Francis, dean of Carlisle, 200, 208

INDEX.

Close, Nicholas, 105
Cockburn, vicar of Brampton, 160
Collinson, Rev. Thomas, 182
—— Thomas, provost of Queen's, 201
Columba, St., dedications to, 35, 36, 38
Comber, dean of Carlisle, 135
Commendation to England of Scotland and Strathclyde, 45
" Comperta," the, 100
Conference, Diocesan, constitution of, 194
—— —— attendance at, 197
Congress Church, at Carlisle, 198
Conisheed, Priory, 228
"Constitutions," new, in the diocese, 97
Convalescent Institution at Silloth, 200
Copes, when used in cathedral, 163
Council of Scottish bishops at Carlisle, 68
Country, nature of, in early times, 10, 15
Court of High Commission, proceedings of, 126
Crosby Ravensworth, litigation as to Church, 77
Cumberland, Lord, 122
—— state of, in 1562, 122
Cumbria, a fief of England, 46
—— chief *rendezvous* of the Danes, 46
—— 28, 29, 46, 47
Cumbri, the, 28
Cuthbert, St., 31, 50, 52
—— at Carlisle, 41, 42
—— translation of his body, 52

Dacre, Lord, 122
Dacre's Raid, 125
Dacre, peace of, 45

Dacre, or Dacor, monastery at, 54, 65
Dægsastan, battle of, 27
Dalston, manor of, granted to bishop of Carlisle, 73
—— litigation as to manor, 74, 79
Dalston, William de, prior of Carlisle, refuses obedience to his bishop, 98
Danish colonisation of Cumbria, 46
Deans, rural, annual meeting of, 198
Deanery, the, 139, 146
Daeth, the Black, 94
Dedications of churches, 23, 32, 33, 36, 38, 50, 52, 53
—— —— lost, 38, 40
Deities, local, 20
—— foreign, 21
Denton, Parish of, 176
Denton, Rev. Thomas, 183
D'Espagnol, Cardinal Peter, at Carlisle, 87
Dethick, chancellor, 209
Dialect, local, 7
Dissent and Church, relations between, 159, 161, 191
—— statistics as to, 185
Dissenting, interest in Carlisle in 1797, 188
Dolphin, 48
Douglas, John, 173, 206
Duncan, king of Scotland, 48
Dunmail, King, 45, 46
Durham, bishops of, claim jurisdiction in Carlisle, 62

Eadred, Lulise, 54
Eardulf, bishop of Lindisfarne, 60
Ecclesiastical interference in politics, 171, 187, 217
Ecgfrid founds nunnery and schools at Carlisle, 59
—— death of, 43

240 CARLISLE.

Edelwan, bishop of Durham, 61
Edmondson, Rev. Thomas, 182
Education Society, Carlisle Diocesan, 192
Educational foundations, 200
Edward the Elder, King of the English, 45
—— the Confessor, 48
Edward I. at Carlisle, 86
—— Holm Cultram, 86
—— Lanercost, 86
—— offers his litter in Carlisle Cathedral, 87
—— dies on Burgh Marsh, 87
Edward II. at Carlisle, 87
—— proclaimed at Carlisle, 88
Elias, archdeacon, 67
Ellenborough, L. C. J., 202
English Conquest, the, 25, 26, 27
—— settlements in the diocese of Carlisle, 30
Episcopalian clergy of Scotland, 183, 184
Ethnological strata, 49
EVERDON, SYLVESTER DE, 62, 75
Executions in Cumberland and Westmorland, 113

FARLAM, PARISH, how plundered, 130, 175
—— church in 1704, 175
Fawcett, Rev. John, 189, 218
Fenris, the Hell-Wolf, 55
Festivities, municipal and ecclesiastical, 136
Firbank chapel, meeting at, 140
FLEMING, SIR GEORGE, 172
Fletcher, chancellor, 212
Fothergill, Thomas, provost of Queen's, 201
Fox, George, 140, 141, 142, 144, 145
Friars, Black or Preachers, 74
—— White or Carmelites, 74

Friars, Grey or Minorites, 74
—— Eremite or Austin, 74
Friends, Society of, 144, 145
Furness Abbey, 228

G., PRIOR OF CARLISLE, 71
Gauls, the, 6
Giant's Grave, the, Penrith, 56
Gibson, bishop of London, 201
Gillesland made pay tribute to Bruce, 88
Gilles, son of Bueth, 63
Gilmore *filius* Gilandi, 61
Gilpin, Bernard, 119, 120, 121
—— Rev. Richard, 139, 146, 151, 153
—— Mr. Recorder William, 159
Glasgow, bishops of, claim jurisdiction in Carlisle, 62
Goidals, the 8
GOODWIN, HARVEY, 173, 200
—— —— Rest Fund, 193, 207
GOODENOUGH, SAMUEL, 173, 186, 187, 190, 206
Gospatric, earl of Northumbria, 48
Gosforth Cross, 55
Gower, Lady, 172
Graham, Dr., dean of Carlisle, 166
Grammar school, see Cathedral school, 139
Grig, 44
Grindal, archbishop, 119, 123, 201
Grisdale, chancellor, 212

HALFDENE, the Danish leader, 44
Halhead Miles, 141
Halifax, Rev. Samuel, 184
HALTON, JOHN DE, 81, 84, 85, 88, 89
—— collector of the tenths in Scotland, 88
Heathenism in Northumbria, attack on, 31
Henry, bishop of Candida Casa, 76

Herbert, St., 50
Hercla, Andrew de, defends Carlisle, 88
Hexham, prior of, hung, 112
—— bishopric of, 63
—— Abbey, 85
Hexhamshire given to see of York, 65
Hilda, St., dedication to, 50
Holm Cultram Abbey, 69
—— —— surrendered, 113, 225
—— —— ravaged by Bruce, 88
Holmes, Thomas, 141
Horncastle, appropriated to bishop of Carlisle, 88, 90
——, John de, elected bishop of Carlisle, 95
Howgill, Francis, 140, 141
Hubbersty, Miles, 141
Hubberthorne, Richard, 141
Hudson, Prebendary, 217
HUGH, 71, 72
Hunsdon, Lord, 124
Hymn-book at Nawork Castle, 117

INCURABLES, HOME FOR, 200
Indulgences, Instances of, 99
Infirmary, Cumberland, 200
Inhabitants, earliest of the diocese, 6, 8
Inhabitants, succession of, 6
Inventory of Vestments, Plates, and Service Books borrowed from Cathedral by Bishop Ross, 91
Irish garrison at Carlisle run away, 156
Irish, the, 6
IRTON, RALPH DE, 78, 79

JACKSON, REV. JOHN, 184
James I. visits Carlisle, 134
James II., addresses to, from the Clergy, 154

Jerby, abbot of Holm Cultram, 111, 113
Jews, stray, 50
John, prior of Carlisle, 71

KENDAL CLERICAL SOCIETY, 191
Kenet or Keneth, St., 39, 54
Kentigern, St., dedications to, 33, 34, 35, 36, 37, 38
King, *de jure* and *de facto*, Bishop Nicolson on, 157
KINGSCOTT, JOHN, 105
Kinneir, Rev. James, 184
KIRKBY, JOHN DE, 92, 93, 94
—— unhorsed in a fight, 93
—— mobbed, 94
KYTE, JOHN, 108, 109

LAMBLEY, NUNNERY at, destroyed, 85
Lanercost Abbey, 85, 93, 226
—— parish of, 176
—— how plundered, 130
Language of Britons or Welsh lingered on, 47
La Rose, *see* ROSE CASTLE.
Larkham, Rev. George, 139, 142, 152, 153
LAW, EDMOND, 173, 202
Law, bishop of Chester, 116
Lectureship at St. Cuthbert's church, 139
——, at cathedral, 140
LEYBURN, ROGER, 105
Linstock Castle, 72, 80, 86, 89
Loki bound, 55, 56
Lollardism, 103
Longevity of the clergy, 182
Lowther, Robert, chancellor, 209
Luguvallium, 18
LUMLEY, MARMADUKE, 104
LYTTLETON, CHARLES, 172, 206

MACBETH, king of Scotland, 48
Magister stolarum, the, 77
MALCLERK, W. DE, 72, 73, 74
Man, Isle of, 47
Marisco, Henry de, prior of Carlisle, 71
Mars, temple to, at Carlisle, 18
Marshall, chancellor, 209
Marston Moor, battle of, 138
Mary Queen of Scots in Carlisle, 123
—— St., the Virgin, dedications to, 53
Melburn appropriated to bishop of Carlisle, 89
MERKS, THOMAS, 100
Meschines, Ranulph de, 66
MEYE, JOHN, 121, 125
Michael, St., dedications to, 53
MILBURN, RICHARD, 131
Milner, Isaac, dean of Carlisle, 187, 189, 208
Missionary Students' Fund, diocesan, 193
Mithras, worship of, 21
Moore, George, 218
—— educational fund, 203
Morpeth, Lord, 191
Mortuaries and probates, 108, 109
Mungo, St., dedications to, 33
Musgrave, Thomas, dean of Carlisle, 155

NAUGHLEY, REV. ALEXANDER, 182
—— Rev. Andrew, 183
Need fire, the, 22
"New learning," the, 110
NICOLSON, WILLIAM, 150, 154, 155, 156, 157, 158, 160, 164, 165, 166, 167, 168, 169, 206, 207
—— his circular to the clergy, 156
—— on conventicles, 154
—— censured by parliament, 171

Nicols, Rowland, chancellor, 209
Nicolson, Joseph, 171
Ninian, St., 23, 24, 32, 64
Nonconformist bodies, their pedigree, 154
Non-jurors, 158
Norfolk, Duke of, proclaims martial law, 112
Norman, sculptured stones, pre- 56
Norse colonisation of Cumbria, 47
North, the rising of the, 123, 125
Northumbria, earls of, 48
—— kingdom of, 26, 30, 44
Nova Taxatio, the, 83, 89, 90

OGHAMS, 56
OGLETHORPE OWEN, 119
OLDRIDGE, ROBERT, 109, 115
Ordination lists, 97
Ordines quatuor, the, 74, 97
OSBALDISTON RICHARD, 172
Oswald, bishop of Raphee, 201
Over Denton, church of, a typical one, 220
—— in what parish, 4
—— parish, how plundered, 130

PRIOR OF CARLISLE, 71
Paley, Dr., archdeacon, 187, 211
Papists, Irish at Carlisle, 155
Parliament of Carlisle, the, 86
Parochial history proposed, 199
—— system, in force early, 61
Pastoral staff, presentation of, to bishop of Carlisle, 198
Paterson, dean of Carlisle, 135
Patrick, St., dedications to, 32
Patrick, son of Culwen, 32
Paulinus, 31
Pearson, Anthony, 141
PENNY, JOHN, 105
PERCY, HUGH, 2, 89, 173, 230, 207
—— WILLIAM, 105
Peredur, the prince of sunshine, 29

Perjury prevalent in diocese of Carlisle, 98
Perkins, Sir Christopher, dean of Carlisle, 121
Petilius Cerealis, 11
Piccolomini, Æneas Sylvius, his account of the country, 106
Pilgrimage of Grace, the, 111, 113
Plate, church, in diocese of Carlisle, 229
Pluralities, prevalence of, 174
Portrait, first, of a bishop of Carlisle 101
POTTER, BARNABY, 131, 133
—— his account of his diocese, 133
Preach, licences to, 152
Preaching competition, 139
Prescott, Archdeacon, 214
Preston, bishop of Ferns, 202
Priors of Carlisle, 71, 208
Probates and mortuaries, 108

QUEEN'S College, Oxford, diocesan connexion with, 203

RAINBOW, EDWARD, 146, 147, 148, 149
Ralph, Flambard, bishop of Durham, 64
Readers, 174, 181
Reged, 28, 47
Registers, episcopal, of Carlisle, 82, 96, 99, 101
REID, ROBERT, 100
Rejoicings at prospect of an heir to James II., 155
Religion of the Britons, 11
—— waves of, 49
Relph, Rev. Josiah, 183
Revolution, clergy uneasy about, 156, 157
Rey Cross on Stainmoor, 63
Rhyderic, 29
Riots in the cathedral, 99

Robert, archdeacon, 67
ROBINSON, HENRY, 121, 130
Robinson, Christopher, executed at Carlisle, 130
—— Jack, 201
Roman conquest of Britain, the, 111
—— wall, the, 14
—— rule, duration of, 14
—— remains, camps, villas, &c., 16, 17, 18, 19
—— cattle fairs, 18
—— roads, 19
—— lapidary remains, 19
—— deities, 20
—— garrisons, the, 25
—— traditions introduced into Cumbria, 41
Romanus, John, archbishop of York, 89
Rose Castle, 74, 104, 109, 146, 147
—— burnt by Bruce, 88
—— who planned by, 89
ROSS, JOHN, 90
Rothbury, William de, archdeacon, 96
Rothelfeld, W. de, elected bishop of Carlisle, 78
Runic inscriptions, 56, 57

SALKELD, Great, rectory, 3
Sancroft, archbishop, declines oath of allegiance, 158
Sandys, archbishop, 119, 201, 216
Sarum, use of, in diocese of Carlisle, 118
Savage, Rev. Arthur, 146, 216
Sawley, abbot of, hung, 112
Saxon sepulchral cross, 52
—— hogbacks, 54
Scaleby, presentment of churchwardens, 1684, 161
School, Central, founded in Carlisle, 190

School, Grammar, and others, 201, 202
—— masters, 181, 184
—— houses, churches used as, 166
SCROPE, RICHARD, 105
SENHOUSE, RICHARD, 131
Servanus, St., 34
Seton nunnery, 228
SEVERN, WILLIAM, 105
Shap Abbey, 227
Singleton, Isaac, chancellor, 209
Siward, earl of Northumberland, 48
SMITH, THOMAS, 146, 150, 154, 159, 161, 201, 216
Smith, Sir Thomas, dean of Carlisle, 121
SNOWDEN, ROBERT, 131
——, his account of his diocese, 131
Snowden, Mrs., 131
Society for Promoting Christian Knowledge, 191
Society for the Propagation of the Gospel, 191
Societies for the suppressing of immorality and profaneness, 159
—— for the Reformation of Manners, 154
Solemn League and Covenant, the, 139
Spiritualities of the diocese of Carlisle, 83
Stapleton church in 1704, 175
Starr, Rev. Comfort, 139, 153
Star of the North, the, 139, 142
Statutes of Cathedral, their validity impugned, 169
"Steeple House," the, Carlisle, 143
STERNE, RICHARD, 146
Stone implements, 7
STORY, EDWARD, 105
—— Thomas, recorder of Pennsylvania, 155
Strathclyde, 28, 29, 43, 47

STRICKLAND, WILLIAM DE, 100, 103, 104
Stycas, Northumbrian, 51
Suffragan bishop, appointment of, 199
Superstitions, peculiar, 22
Sword of honour, the mayor's, 139

TAIT, Dean, 208
Taxatio, the, of Pope Nicholas, 83
—— in Scotland, 83
Temporalities of diocese of Carlisle, 83
Tenew, 34
Teviotdale, falls to see of Glasgow, 65
Theodore, of Tarsus, 31
Theologic Prelector, 140
Thor, 55, 56
Thomas, bishop of Rochester, 202
Todd, Prebendary, 166, 169, 170, 216
Towneley, chancellor of Carlisle, 111
Tremellius, John Emanuel, 216
Triermain, chapel of, 61
Trumwine, bishop, 43
Tuda, bishop, 57
Tullie, Thomas, dean and chancellor, 147, 155, 160, 202
—— Rev. Timothy, 139
Tyson, Rev. Edward, 182

USHER, archbishop, 135

Vacancy of Ministers, the 132
Valor Ecclesiasticus of Henry VIII., 83
Veredictum Antiquorum, 61, 219
VERNON [HARCOURT], EDWARD VENABLES, 173, 186
Verus Valor, the, 83
Vespasian, 11
Vetus Valor, the, 83

VILLIERS, HENRY MONTAGUE, 173, 201
VIPONT or VETERIPONT, THOMAS, 75
Visitations in diocese of Carlisle, history of, 213
—— of the cathedral, 170

WALDEGRAVE, SAMUEL, 173, 193, 207
Walker, Rev. Robert (wonderful Walker), 174, 182
Walter, prior of Carlisle, 71
—— a wealthy Norman, 66
Watson, bishop of Llandaff, 202
WAUGH, JOHN, 171, 201
Waugh, Chancellor, 172, 210
Wealas, the, 26
Weddings, Gretna Green, 213
Well, Roman, at Carlisle, 42, 43
Welsh kingdoms, the, 27
WELTON, GILBERT DE, bishop of Carlisle, 95
West, Rev Lewis, 138, 145
Wetheral Abbey, 69

Wetheral Priory, 224
—— —— surrendered, 114
WHELPDALE, ROGER, 104
WHITE, FRANCIS, dean of Carlisle, 131, 135
Whitehead, George, 141
Whitherne, 23
Widows and Orphans, Society for Relief of necessitous, 191
Wigs, when last worn, 187
Wilfrid of York, 31
—— St., dedication to, 53
Wilkinson, Priest, 142, 143
William and Mary, proclaimed at Carlisle, 156
Wills, local, 96
Wilson, Sir J., 201
Woden and Thor, heathenism of, 47, 49, 50
Wooley, Sir John, dean of Carlisle, 121
Wren, Gawen, 153, 154

Yates, Sir Joseph, 201